AND SO IT WAS

AS I RECALL

AND

SO IT WAS

AS I RECALL

Rose M. Thomas

Salt Cellar Press

Revised Edition

Copyright © 2000 by Rose M. Thomas

Salt Cellar Press,
2311 Covenanter Dr., Bloomington, IN 47401

ISBN 0-9706822-1-2

PRINTED IN THE UNITED STATES OF AMERICA

Cover design by S.S. Thomas

Dedication

To my children, grandchildren and my extended
family members who listened and were instructed
by these stories.

Acknowledgments

The author and publisher wishes to thank all the librarians, reviewers and others whose advice made this revision possible.

Table of Contents

Chapter One

The Store

My father's general store was my whole early life and home. The family lived above and behind it. The large, decorative concrete block building was as wide as the business lot, with two front entrances. The smaller left entrance to the side opened upon a stairway leading to the upper living quarters. The recessed main entrance was flanked by two large store display windows, sheltered by a roll down canvas awning which ran the width of the store front. This main door had an electrical bell system which buzzed in the back of the store and was clearly heard in the house whenever the door would open. In addition the door carried a spring-hung silver bell that tinkled sweetly as the door moved back and forth.

When customers walked into the store, they would see on their left a beautiful, long mahogany counter stretching from the front display case to the rear of the store. Behind it, stretching from the wooden floor to the tin ceiling, were shelves packed with gallons and half gallons of the golden cans of Bertolli olive oil, Progresso oil and other oils; pound tins of Hershey's cocoa; canned coffees; tins of baking soda and baking powders; vanilla, almond, anise and other extracts; and a smattering of "modern" convenience foods, mainly canned peas and tomatoes.

Most families prepared their meals using fresh

produce.   During the winter, people bought those vegetables which could be stored easily- like carrots, potatoes, cabbage and squash.

The glass display case near the entrance, about counter high, held cartons of all the cigarettes of that period as well as boxes of cigars of all kinds. The smoking of an Italian stogie, of the twisted cheroot style, nearly did me in one summer day.

Another case on top of the mahogany counter with a slanted glass front and glass shelves held most of the breads, cakes and confections, including the popular red and white Jordan almond candies used in celebrating christenings and weddings. Additional fresh breads were stacked on top and to the side of this case. Long French and Italian breads were displayed in artfully hand made bushel baskets.

The beautiful counter was so long it also comfortably held a Toledo scale, a cutting frame holding butcher paper for wrapping purchases, a lavishly ornamented brass National cash register, and a bookkeeping cabinet with a check writing machine.

The right side of the store shelved the dry goods, paper products, a few more canned goods and cereals. Coming forward to the front, all the fresh produce was displayed. The center of the store was occupied by what could not be put on the shelves. There were barrels of dried black Greek and Italian olives, as well as large, plump, shiny green olives swimming in brine; cases of dried cod fish (baccala), and golden smoked chub;   smaller kegs of pickled herring, varieties of sardines and anchovies. On the wide planked floor, covered with fresh clean sawdust, there were displayed open burlap bags of dried large Roman, lupine and other beans. Nearby there were huge glass jars of whole cucumber pickles, pickled pigs feet, and pickled eggs. There were wooden boxes filled with almonds, hazelnuts, English walnuts, pecans, and fresh chestnuts from Italy, too. Rings of dried figs from Greece and boxes of dates, raisins, apricots and other dried fruit all found space in the store.

The meat case, located several feet from the back wall, was tickled from above by the hanging whole large, medium and small balls and purse styles of cheese; whole, dried hanging salami and prosciuttos. The refrigerated interior displayed cut meats: wonderfully smoked hams, capocollo, salami, supre satta, pepperoni, prosciutto, mortedella, head cheese, and sausages, hot or sweet with fennel. Customers would also see cut cheeses: Roquefort, gorgonzola, Swiss, brick, provolone, Parmesan, Romano, Pecorini and others like the creamy ricotta that I still love. When a housewife walked into this world, it was a little bit of heaven. The combination of the sights - sounds and smells lifted her spirits and became etched happily into her memory. Then, it was part of the good life. Today, its called aroma therapy.

Natural day light illuminated the store, entering through the two large front display windows and several square windows near the ceiling. This was supplemented by a hanging bank of six lightoliers. The 20 foot high ceiling was covered with embossed panels of tin which curved about ten inches down the walls. The white painted patterns swirled off into intricate designs that could mesmerize one who stared at them too long.

On hot summer days, large black oscillating General Electric fans moved the air and cooled the area. Long strands of varied colored paper were tied to the fan grills and would blow outward when the fan was turned on. One or two fans always blew over the boxes of fruit in the front display window. Several others were placed high on the recessed ledges of the square windows near the ceiling, providing cooling. During the cold of winter, the store was warmed by a natural gas radiant style heater. Auxiliary heat came from an electric glow cone element heater.

The back wall of the store was stacked with over one hundred wooden, two foot long boxes that accommodated that length of spaghetti and other pastas. Each box contained 20 (or was it 24) pounds of any kind of pasta one could think of, from different pastinas; Stella, Alphabet, Rings, Semi de Melone, Orzo, Rosa Marina, Acini Di Pepe, Ditalini and Tubetini (used in salads, soups and Pasta e Fagoli); to the pastas like Farfalle, Shells, folded and straight Egg Noodles in several widths, Rigatoni (smooth and rigate), Lasagna, Ziti, Manicotti, the curled Vermicelli, Fussili, Perciatelli, Macaroncelli, Bucatini, Margarita, Mafalda; and of course, Spaghetti and Linguini (regular, medium and thin) , Capellini and Angel Hair pasta. During the Depression, this stock dwindled to about a dozen boxes of the most popular pastas and pastinas.

On the front of each pasta box, a colorful label would display a number along with the name of the pasta. The thinner the pasta the smaller the number. Most likely they would run from Capellini, No. 1, to maybe No. 60 for Lasagna. If a customer asked for a pasta by name, my Father would find it by number. It was amazing how he, who could read only a little, would do this quickly by the number on the box without ever missing. He knew his figures well though, and was very quick and accurate in his calculations.

During the years preceding the Great Depression, every bit of our store and the large store room of the building next door were filled to overflowing with all sorts of inventory. Even the two story house located behind the store as well as our large separate garage served as warehouses. Non-family employees were hired to help with the very successful business.

One of our favorite spots as children was the Nabisco cookie rack, of course. It held a dozen or so cartons that were regularly refilled with sweet treats. I remember the coconut covered pink or white marshmallow cookies; yum! And those that were encased in chocolate; yum, yum! The square cartons, about a foot cubed, had a metal frame with a glass door in front so that one could easily enjoy "just looking" for a while at each of all the varieties.

There were also the green coffee beans that would be roasted in a black metal cylinder set in a solidly framed, metal stand. Father or Mother would slowly turn the cylinder by its side handle over a medium gas flame, tumbling the beans until they were of the proper color and aroma. Different varieties of beans were ground for special orders. Ah, the aroma! I remember how wonderful this roasting coffee smelled especially when it was brewing in the early morning. Coffee, while its aroma was delightful, never tasted as delicious as the aroma seemed to promise. As a young girl, I could never drink it. It was not until many, many years later, after I started working, that I began to drink coffee, mostly due to economics. At coffee breaks during the day, I would go with fellow office workers to a nearby diner where the hot, bitter coffee was five cents a cup, while a serving of milk was ten cents a glass. Everyone drank and seemed to enjoy their coffee. Though I preferred milk, I also wanted to save that extra nickel. Therefore, from time to time I would try to drink coffee with lots of cream and sugar. It took years before I could finish a full cup. I wasted many nickels on cups of coffee that I only tasted but could not drink.

The wonderful arrangements filling the wooden display boxes and baskets of fruits and vegetables graced the store like paintings. Customers didn't "pick through the produce like chickens" but were waited on. The produce was carefully selected, usually by Father or Mother, weighed and put in proper size brown bags for the customers. Then the display would be rearranged to look its best for the next customer. Even potatoes, onions and garlic, artfully arranged, added to the delightful scene.

The main counter that ran almost the length of the store was a marvel to me. Built into its front were ten displays of popular pastinas encased in recesses behind glass windows. The recesses were about 6" high x 12" long x 1" deep. The rich dark mahogany counter made a most attractive background for these displays. Children especially loved to scrunch down and scoot along the floor naming the various pastinas, pointing out what their favorite of that day was.

On the clerk's side of the counter, opposite the displays, there were large deep drawers that held about 20 pounds of the various pastinas. The customer would look at the displays at the front of the counter and usually make several selections like five pounds of Acini di Pepe, three pounds of Rosa Marina and a pound of Stellas. The pastinas would be put into three separate brown bags of the appropriate size, weighed, then tied with string to insure no possible spillage.

My earliest memories of the store are of the constant comings and goings of customers, of a steady flow of their gossip and conversations between them and my parents. The store was my gateway to the world as well as the door into my home.

Chapter II

Living Quarters

From behind the counter at the rear of the store, we could either go up or down. Going up a few steps we would enter the living room and an equally long dining room, then the kitchen and back porch.

If we went down, we would go into a basement area of three rooms. The floors were all concreted and a water drain was located in the center of each room. A service sink near the basement entrance was used for washing produce before its placement on display, and for whatever else needed washing.

One side basement room was filled with coal delivered through a small side window near the top of the wall adjacent to the driveway. This always was a dusty and dirty job. The central basement room had a large, pot-bellied cast iron stove connected to the chimney with a short flue, but it was not cased and had no heat ducts. The red hot stove, being uncased, simply radiated the heat out into this room.

The heated air rose up through a large decorative, square register in the floor located just above the stove. Along with the rising hot air would come smoke and fine ash, which occurred at those times when the stove was fed its ration of coal, or when ashes were removed. The film of dirt from this and from the industrial smoke from the factories in the surrounding area meant that we had to deep clean constantly. We also got a lot of fall-out from Pittsburgh, known for many years as one of the dirtiest American cities. Oh, what all were we breathing?

Every spring, one of the extra chores was to wash down the main floor's walls with rags, hand sponges, Climaline (a water softener), and Oxydol or the Gold Dust Twins soap powders. A very dramatic difference would be seen immediately between the washed and the unwashed walls.

Curtains were washed, starched and stretched to dry on collapsible wooden frames that adjusted to size. Stretching the curtains over the many metal points, sticking straight up, was always a little hazardous. When putting the curtains on, we would prick our fingers now and then. When in use the frame was on legs which could be adjusted to stand much like an easel. When not in use, the entire frame was disassembled and stored, ready for the next seasonal cleaning.

From the living room, a long flight of stairs led up to the bedrooms, and a bathroom complete with footed tub, wash basin and toilet. Early Monday mornings, 4:30 or 5 a.m., the bathroom doubled as our laundry room. The Maytag washing machine was rolled in from one of the adjacent rooms and pushed up against the tub.

I considered Monday to be the worst day of the week. We woke to the sound of the groaning washer. The bathroom now was not private because, with the Maytag there, the door could not be closed. I felt guilty that Mother had to be the one burdened with this laundry task for the eight or so hours while we were in school, in addition to taking care of her usual tasks in the kitchen as well as the store. During the summer and when we were not in school, my sister and I helped with the laundry.

There was no need for women of that era to join exercise classes or walking clubs. The old-fashioned washboard was used a great deal for hand-scrubbing clothes throughout the week. We got more than enough exercise; bending up and down over the tub, carrying bushels of laundry to hang out to dry, scrubbing floors, cleaning, etc. The four mile hike to our garden did us much good, too.

Laundry Monday! The washer was filled with hot water, soap and bleach. White shirts, sheets, and other white clothing made up the initial loads. After being washed for the appropriate time, these clothes were put through the washer's wringer, dropping into the tub half filled with hot, clean rinse water. The clothes were hand rinsed. With the wringer put on reverse, laundry was put back through the wringer, ending up on the lid of the washing machine.

That first rinse water was drained out and the tub refilled with clean water. The shirts were returned to the tub of fresh water and individually swished around for their last rinse. The progressively darker colored loads of laundry were wrung out into once-used rinse water, swished about individually, and again put back through the wringer. The twice used

20

rinse water was drained and fresh water added for the next second rinse.

After each load had been put back through the wringer, Mother placed them in bushel baskets that she carried out to the second floor porch. There she hung them with clothes pins on clotheslines strung out on pulleys over the garden to a telephone pole in the corner of the yard. Extra lines crisscrossed the porch to carry the heavy, sturdier clothes from trousers to rags and rugs. This went on all morning, until every bit of laundry for the nine people in our family was done.

Then there was all the mending of the clean clothes and baskets full of ironing. When we were old enough, and we soon became old enough, my sisters and I ironed our own clothes first, then pillowcases, and finally most everything. Mother would never let any of us iron Father's white shirts though; they had to be just so.

Mother started ironing as soon as the first load of shirts were nearly dry, continuing all day Monday and Tuesday. Normally about a bushel full of torn laundry was set aside to be mended and buttons replaced after the regular ironing was done. Ironing was finished sometime on Wednesday. As was the rule in those days, the boys did not iron anything and did almost none of the household chores.

The bed rooms were spread over the entire building. Our parents had a sitting room next to their bedroom. Several rooms were used to store things like the washing machine, curtain stretchers and dirty laundry. A central hall held the gas heater used to heat all the rooms on the top floor.

I was born in my parent's front bedroom, one cold day in January. Funny, I don't remember what happened, even though I was present at the time.

Chapter III

The Old Neighborhood

While the depression days still are most vivid; I also remember, fleetingly, the more prosperous days when the store would be crowded with customers from the surrounding boroughs and towns. Father had one of the most complete ethnic grocery stores in the county. People came to buy, enjoy samples, visit, see and be seen in this bustling haven.

Housewives would love to come in to be entertained and kid with Father asking, "Hey Joe! How much for the lemons today?" He would return the tease and delight them with a ditty:

"Two for a nickel. Three for a dime. Six for a quarter all of the time."

Our immediate neighborhood was made up of families from Greek, Polish, Jewish, Hungarian, Syrian, Italian, Irish, Russian and English origins. There were no solid clusters of any one nationality; all lived, sprinkled about next to each other, enjoying the fruits of their diversity. A few of the black families, as I recall, lived in company houses several blocks away. Several other black families lived in the more well-to-do part of town.

I have no recollection of any cultural problems

whatsoever; nor any hateful actions by any one group against another. Of course, each ethnic group took pride in their traditions and food specialties which they happily shared with all.

When my Syrian friend shared her delicious "kibbe" with me, she insisted it was the best food in the world. Baklava was the greatest food in the world according to my Greek friend and so on and so on. My closest friends, who came into in our big yard almost daily, were Greek, Syrian, Italian and Hungarian. We played Hide and Go Seek; Go Shippy Go; Kick, Kick the Can; Hop Scotch; Jump Rope; Farmer in the Dell; Ring Around the Rosie; Go In and Out the Window as well as other round games.

My older sister and brother, with their friends, would make up plays that we all would perform or attend. They were the oldest children in the group, so usually got their way. One play I remember required only one male and one female role. This play was impossible to forget, because they liked to perform it over and over and over each year, for a number of years, by their request only. My sister and brother liked being the stars, while I and everyone else were the audience, as well as the chorus. The rest of us became rather tired of it and sometimes ignored it all, until we could join in the funeral procession of their musical tragedy. Or, were we talking opera here?

The play went like this. The heroine shyly sat on the top step of the downstairs porch. The hero, swaggering somewhat, sauntered over carrying a large cigar made of rolled up newspaper. He climbed the few stairs and sat at the heroine's feet, pretending to "smoke his cigar". All the audience-chorus would sing:

He sat down beside her,
Smo-king a cigar,
Smo-king a cigar,
Smo-oh-king a ci-gar-ar.

He said that he loved her,
Um-humm, he did,
Um-humm, he did,
Um-humm-um, he di-i-i-d.

They were to get married,
But then she died,
But then she died,
But - then she di-i-ed

We went to her funeral,
(audience / chorus in single file procession)
Boo hoo we cried,
Boo hoo we cried,
Booo hoo we cri-i-ed.

THE END!!!!

The two stars usually had to remind us that we all were supposed to clap at the end.

Of course, there were other funerals for birds, lightning bugs, and even queen ants. Usually we used little boxes like penny matchboxes to put them in. We cried and prayed over them, then they were buried in the garden. Never did mosquitoes or flies get this treatment or respect.

What a relief it was from those somber funeral dramas to hear the booming of a BIG drum. We knew it was the Salvation Army coming down to our street corner to sing and pray for us all. I remember the neat uniforms of the men and the red beribboned bonnets of their ladies with huge wide puffed up bows tied next to their faces. How sharp! It was so grand just to look at them.

One of their songs made a lasting impression on me. It was about the devil and was a favorite of us all. Having heard it many times, we would wait anxiously each time to hear it and sing along with this small band from the Salvation Army. We did so with gusto; complete with the appropriate devil shooting motions.

The song went something like this:

The Salvation Army has the right to beat the drum,
The tambourin-er too, to make the devil run,
Oh come (inviting arm motions here)
and join our Army
and get a bashful gun,
And SHOOT (pretending to shoot with rifle)

the nasty devil,
If you want to see him run."

After a few holy words and a prayer, one of their people would take up a collection using a tambourine as an offering plate. Upon gathering only the usual few coins from the grownups, they would sing several more songs; then depart as they had come, with their drum booming away, to another corner of town to save more souls.

The Army's time at our corner was always too short. We wished they would stay much longer and come back more often. After all, there was no television for us to watch and we could rarely get a dime to pay for the movies. This was good, real live musical drama that came right up to our own street corner, where we were able to join in with them a bit. It was a great diversion from our summer boredom.

This was not the only taste of a religion other than our own. Miners' Hall was a large gray two story wooden building about half a block from our home. The main floor was kept for the coal miners' use and their meetings. But the large upstairs hall was rented out to the public from time to time.

There was no black church in town, nor do I recall there being any such church many years later. So the black folk of the surrounding area rented that large upstairs area for their Sunday evening church services. When the windows were open on hot summer nights, their voices would sing out and they could be heard for many blocks across the town. Neighbors sat on their porches, enjoying the inspired singing. This lively and fervent congregation could match or better any of today's gospel singers. Of that, I am sure.

One such Sunday evening after the sun had set, several of us, having dared and double-dared each other, summoned up enough courage to quietly, cautiously, climb up the steep, narrow, outside stairway. We sat just below the top landing where we felt that no one in the congregation would see us.

In the dusk, we listened and took turns now and then peeking in to watch this rather 'strange' gathering of 30 or so people. The singing went on with emotion and swaying motion, the likes of which we had never seen or heard; not even in the few movies we'd been able to see. There were many punctuations of *Amen* and *Hallelujah*, accompanied by much hand clapping. We were moved to join in; but instead, controlled ourselves and kept quiet so as not to be discovered by any of the congregation.

I remember being fascinated by the women (sisters) who wore white dresses and very large white kerchiefs that covered their hair and forehead and tied at the back of their heads. Their white attire extended down to white hose and shoes. The rest of the congregation sang, listened to readings and preaching. Some had their feet washed as depicted in Bible readings.

At some point, we were discovered sitting there

on the darkened stairway. A most kindly gentlemen, perhaps their preacher, invited and urged us to come in, have a seat and to join them in prayer. But I was too shy for that and quickly scampered home, as did everyone else. On other Sunday evenings, we did return to sit, listen and peek in from the top of that darkened stairway into the religious world of these people that we never knew.

This neighborhood no longer exists. It was almost completely destroyed during the lowest point of the depression when people lost their property because they could not pay their property taxes. Through the Sheriff's Sales, the local town and county agencies seized the neighboring Greek Coffee House, the Syrian Dry Goods Store, the Italian Restaurant, and many similar, family-run businesses for unpaid taxes. These buildings were left empty or replaced by pool rooms and other nonproductive operations. No children replaced our friends (some 20 children). They were gone to us forever; moving in with relatives in other towns and states.

What a cruel ridiculous, stupid move on the part of the government. On the one hand, government handed out relief to people who were down and out. Yet, on the other hand, they would not allow hard-working, honest people the dignity of struggling through this phase until they could pay their taxes. The government did not gain that much either. The new tenants did not stay long, paying little or no taxes. Many of the places were simply boarded up.

Chapter IV

DOCTOR - DOCTOR

Three little children jumping on the bed,
One fell off and broke his head,
Mama called the doctor, and Doctor said,
"That's what you get for jumping on the bed."

Not so! Mother almost never called the doctor. We had to take care of almost all illnesses and accidents ourselves. To tell all the mishaps and illnesses suffered in a family of nine, would take volumes; so I will relate mainly to what involved me over my younger years.

True, a doctor was called for each birth of the seven children in our family. Thank goodness there were no major problems or still births that I knew of. But my Mother, being just a petite lady under five feet, did undoubtedly have a difficult time. We were never told anything connected with births. I remember hearing her scream at the times of the actual births of my younger brothers and sister. We were quickly sent off to play in the back yard or downstairs, until the doctor was finished doing whatever he had to do. We decided that my Mother was yelling because she wanted a baby. When the doctor brought one, she'd stop yelling and screaming.

So, the sounds from Mother's bedroom did not

upset us unduly. We felt that when they ended there would be this wonderful new baby.

Dr. Wilson delivered nearly all the children of our family. Once, as he was hurrying upstairs we stopped him and asked about the new baby he was bringing to our family. He said the baby was in his black bag. Of course, our next question was to ask whether we were getting a baby girl or a baby boy. He told us that it was a baby girl. When we kept tugging and begging to see the baby, he said he couldn't do that because Mother had to be the first to see her.

It wasn't too long before we found out that the doctor was right. It was a baby girl. Since the doctor was able to tell us downstairs before he saw Mother, that he had a baby girl for us, the baby must have been born before he arrived. Undoubtedly as soon as Dr. Wilson arrived at our door, Father told him that he and my Godmother had already delivered a baby girl.

Many years later I overheard Father's conversation with my grown sister regarding the births of several of our babies. He complained that even though Dr. Wilson had his home office just a block or so away, one of the few cars in town, and was alerted in more than enough time; he still didn't arrive in time. So it was Father who, with the help of my Godmother, delivered those babies.

Father said Mother never went to the doctor's office for pre-natal exams or consultations for any of her babies. She only saw the doctor at the time of delivery. Whether he did or did not deliver the babies,

Dr. Wilson still billed his $25 delivery fee. Father didn't think that was right but paid the fee anyway.

When I was about to be born on that very cold day in January, Dr. Wilson was not in town. Dr. Boes (a tall, slim man) came to deliver me, the only one in the family not delivered by Dr. Wilson or Father. The doctors were two very different personalities. Dr. Wilson was a very outgoing, happy type person; Dr. Boes was a serious man of few words.

Shortly after being born I developed problems. The doctor said he could do nothing more for me; that I would not live. The parish priest was called to baptize me and administer the last rites. Years later my Godmother related to me the events of my birth. She told me Mother carried me to the sitting room adjoining their bedroom. Throughout the night she cried, rocked and prayed without stopping. At some point I began to turn blue. Suddenly, I coughed up some sort of a clot. From that point on things got better and my first worldly crisis was over. I had become the fourth child. Over the years two more brothers and then another sister were born, and I became the middle child in this family of seven.

Well, there have been times, when I thought that if I had died at birth, I would, without a doubt, be in heaven. But with all the past and future possibilities of doing something wrong, who knows where I will end up. Everyone says that there must be reasons for me to have lived on and on. It has been an extremely busy life with many more crisis. Let's get back to doctors and such now.

Going into first grade, as a requirement by the school's health code, I was vaccinated for smallpox by Dr. Boes. This vaccination did not take and the school nurse was skeptical that I ever was vaccinated. Well, I had to show evidence of a vaccination by developing that pus filled sore on the upper part of my left arm that every one else got in those days as a result of this medical benefit. So I returned to Dr. Boes for another arm laceration and health preservative. Well, the next inoculation did not take, nor did the next.

Finally, the school nurse gave up and accepted a note from the doctor that I had indeed been given the vaccine several times and so permitted me to stay in school. After I was married and had several children, their pediatrician, Dr. Steinman, of Ithaca, NY, said she would give me a vaccination that definitely would take. I submitted to this fourth treatment. No; I still don't have a vaccination mark on my arm.

We did not receive tetanus shots either. Our many cuts and bad gashes were usually washed and soaked in hot salt water, then sometimes touched up with iodine, or else they healed on their own. One day, I remember being adventurous with a friend and taking the long route home from school without Mother's permission. We climbed through a barbed wire fence to save some time and somehow, the rusty barb on the fence dug into my leg, tearing out a chunk of my flesh. Well, I shouldn't have taken that way home, so I said nothing about it, but doctored myself as best I could. It left quite a scar, staying visible for many years. Today, it's nearly impossible to see.

Another hideous scar was on the wrist of my left hand, just below my thumb. I had jumped down the short flight of stairs from our living room to pick up the ringing phone in the store below. We had been waiting for a brother in the Navy who was much overdue for his birthday home coming. I was very anxious about that call. As I held on to the half-door and jumped, a nail head sticking up at that corner ripped across my wrist, leaving an inch long, jagged gash there. I repeatedly cleansed and soaked the gash in hot salt water. No doctor this time either. Another prominent scar was notched into the yard stick of my life's measure, but as ugly as it was, it is hardly visible today.

Many times I went to school without saying I was not feeling well. Then in the third grade, I really did it. I came down with scarlet fever. I was so ill I could not hold my head up or hardly stand and certainly could not go to school.

At first I was so weak I didn't know or care about anything. But, as I became stronger, I was anxious to go back to school for I loved school and always did very well. Most of the peeling from the awful scarlet fever rash was gone in a few weeks and I felt I was strong enough to go back to school. My parents thought I was too impatient and kept me home a while longer. But every day I pressed and pleaded to go back to school. My parents finally relented.

The school nurse checked me, and when she saw the remains of the scaling skin, she checked my brothers and sister. The nurse said that I had had scarlet fever and that since my sister and I slept together in the same bed, she surely had it, too. Sister protested saying she was feeling fine and didn't have and didn't want scarlet fever.

We and our brothers were sent home and a quarantine sign was put on our house. People were dying from scarlet fever and quarantines seemed to be the way to curb its spread. No one could come to visit us nor could we go anywhere for, I believe it was, 30 days. Sister wasn't very happy with me for what I had caused everyone to be put through. She let me know this more than once. .

Many a night while sharing our bed she would pinch me over and over until as I moved away I would fall out of bed.

My Mother was very upset about having the quarantine sign put on our house, and I felt I had disgraced the family. As contagious as it was, neither my sister nor my brothers got scarlet fever. It appears that I truly was the sickly one and, as Mother said, caught everything that came along. Unfortunately, my brothers and sister were out of school all that time for nothing and I was out even longer with the real thing.

The following summer, when I was about eight years old, my two older brothers and I were to have our tonsils and adenoids removed. This was because I had had too many illnesses and my brothers apparently had throat problems. We were told that when the operation was over, we would be getting lots of ice cream and Jello. These were *very* rare treats in those days, so it gave us something good to look forward to.

Rather than drive, Father took us by interurban streetcar to Pittsburgh an hour away. There we transferred to a local streetcar that took us to Children's Hospital, another half hour away. We were checked in and my brothers went together to the boy's section, while I was put in a girl's ward. After a short time Father could no longer stay with us and returned home by streetcar.

That evening our Aunt and Uncle, who lived in nearby Mt. Washington, came by incline and streetcar to visit us for a while. They too reminded us that we could have lots of the rare, delicious treats of ice cream and Jello. Aunt and Uncle left too soon; for it was a scary night for this eight year old in that hospital room. I tried thinking of all the funny and good things I could imagine; but not even the thought of all the ice cream and Jello, everyone kept telling me I would get afterwards, made me feel any better.

Morning came and I was taken to the operating room. There was no one there that I knew. I had never seen or met any of the doctors or nurses.   After I was given a few whiffs of ether, I saw whirling figures, heard strange noises and had odd feelings. I thought this must be like what it is to die. I must be dying. No one had prepared me for what I might expect. So, I straightened my sheets, said my prayers and waited to die.

Instead I suddenly found myself back in my hospital bed with a whale of a sore throat. I certainly didn't want to swallow anything, not even that ice cream or Jello that was supposed to be so easy to swallow. And I sure didn't think the operation was easy or painless. Later that afternoon Father returned to take the three of us home, again the two hours by streetcar, to recuperate.

My two brothers did fine. The younger one's adenoid operation discovered he had a Red Cross button lodged in his nose. Apparently that had been the cause of his open-mouthed breathing and terrible smelling breath.

A strange malady affected me during the time I was in the fifth grade. Our teacher was known to drive her top notch class very strictly and without humor. She spent little time in giving assistance or showing understanding for any other than the best students. I started her class as one of the top students. But sometime during that fall, I found myself fumbling along. My right arm would not respond to my wishes. I had difficulty doing ordinary things like tying my shoes, buttoning my clothes, or even putting a spoon to my mouth. It was hard even to hold a pencil properly, and writing became a slow and painful process.

My hand writing began to look like first grade writing, large, shaky and open. In the time it took me to struggle through the spelling of just one word, the rest of the class would have written many. It was especially hard for me during spelling drills, where the teacher would dictate the words out loud to us, separately and in sentence form. I knew the spelling words as well as every one else, but in trying to keep up with the teacher's dictation, I would leave some words unfinished, and omit others. All these incomplete words and omissions were marked as errors, resulting in very low scores for me that year. In oral spelling I had no problems. Because of this sudden collapse in my school performance, I was sent to the school nurse.

The nurse and Mother looked at my hand and arm. But they could see no indication of any trouble. They asked me what was wrong. I did not know. I struggled along, and eventually, what ever it was seemed to work itself out. Never again though did my right arm or hand function as easily as they once did. Naturally this did not make for the happiest of times that school year. I no longer maintained the top grades I had the previous years. While I didn't pass to Grade A-6, I did pass to B-6.

When I was about 17, I did spend a week or so in our local General Hospital. The heating element of the hot water tank had broken. In order to take my bath, I boiled water in our big kettle. It was very heavy and I should have asked for help; but I didn't. As I climbed the stairs with this heavy kettle, I slipped near the top landing. I fell, and the scalding water spilled all over my face and body. My left eye quickly swelled shut. I ran up and down the hall in agony. Mother ripped my button down, red and white checkered acetate dress from me. The large, inch and a half, white buttons scattered everywhere.

Dr. Wilson was called to the house. I was covering my left eye with my hands and kept crying, "My eye, my eye!" I asked if I would ever be able to see with it again. He checked me, said nothing, and ordered an ambulance to take me to the local hospital. No family member was allowed to come with me. I heard the ambulance drivers whispering about how bad my burns were - worse than the woman they took in last week that had died. With the raw, agonizing pain that I had, I wished and wished to die before we got to the next corner.

In my hospital room there was an older women who kept saying over and over, "My, my, my; I never saw *anything* so bad. You sure is gonna be scarred bad - real bad." I pretended to be asleep and not hear her. There was no reason for me to converse with this stranger who was staring at me while spouting such news.

Later that woman went down the hall and brought a friend back to confirm what she diagnosed. Holding out her arm and pointing at me, she told her friend, "Look at her, she's burned worse off than Elsie Anders; isn't she?" Shaking her head her friend quickly agreed. My room mate continued, "Elsie has some great big scars and this one is gonna have worse ones. They'll be real bad, poor thing!" Agreement again, from the friend.

That evening, a dozen or so of my friends circled my bed, with others even standing out in the hall. I must have been a frightening sight; something monstrous to see. Perhaps I looked like one of those beings in the Frankenstein movies, that were in their heyday at that time.

A few days later, my Godmother came to visit me. Abruptly, she asked if I had seen myself. When I replied I had not; she pulled out a mirror and told me to see what I looked like (with my one open eye). "Get used to it," she said, "for you are going to be badly scarred". So, that was that, there wasn't much I could do about it; at least my right eye could see.

But, Dr. Wilson had been an air force doctor and treated many burn victims of fiery plane crashes. Some of the nurses in this hospital didn't think his treatment was proper, others felt it might work. Since all the nurses were not carrying out the Doctor's instructions; they were told to give me all the cocoa butter I wanted to use. For days I spread cocoa butter over all the burns myself, almost non-stop. I probably used up more cocoa butter during that period than the whole hospital used during a year.

What else could I do? I certainly couldn't see

very well with my one eye, there was no radio in the room, and in those days no television. I didn't want to have any conversations with the other person in my room if I could help it. Nurses never would have had or taken the time to do half as much as I did for myself. There were no coverings or other dressings used for any of my burns, just a lot of cocoa butter.

Slowly, day by day, my left eye began to open and the burned skin on my face and body began to peel off. I was red and raw all over. When I returned home weeks later, I continued using the cocoa butter, and as a result, there were no scars. I got glasses for the first time to help with my left eye, which never fully opened for a number of years.

After that, I kept out of the sun, for any sunlight would make my skin smart and it would become quite red. Sunning never was my cup of tea, so not going out into the sun was no great loss for me. Those days of walking the four miles to and from the garden in the country gave me enough sun for several lifetimes. Today, we are cautioned about all the harm too much sun can cause.

Years later, when I was earning my own money, I saved enough to pay for an operation to have a small cyst (one I had since birth) removed from the middle of my chest. I talked to Dr. Wilson. He did not charge me anything for this consultation. Today most doctors charge simply to say 'hello'. Dr. Wilson suggested that I go to Children's Hospital in Pittsburgh to have this done on an out-patient basis.

After he told me how to get there by streetcar, he phoned the hospital and made arrangements for me to be admitted.

There at the hospital several doctors, whom I had never seen or talked to before, came in and looked me over. They called in a few more residents to look me over as well. I was prepared for surgery. Somebody cut out what needed to be cut out; somebody else put in the stitches. I know, because I was not fully unconscious.

Shortly after this was done and when I was no longer groggy, I was discharged to return home as I had come, on a series of street car transfers.

At the proper time I went back to the hospital to have the stitches removed by yet another doctor. So much for modern medicine. Looking at myself, I saw that the cyst was indeed gone; but instead there was a more prominent, ugly scar, three or four times larger than the cyst had been. It remains to this day. So it goes; another notch in my yardstick.

Most of the rest of my doctoring relates to the birth of my five children. As there was nothing medically extraordinary about those events, let me go on to another topic for the time being.

Chapter V

The Best Teacher Ever

In those days, when you missed school, assignments were not sent home to you. You simply lost everything to do with school. I was absent for more than six weeks altogether in the third grade because of the scarlet fever, and so didn't know whether I would be passed up to the fourth grade.

After talking back and forth; my third grade teacher, Mrs. Beatty, and the fourth grade teachers, Miss Aubrey and Miss Berger, decided that, since I had always been an honor roll student; they would pass me. But I could not pass to Miss Aubrey's A-4 as my brothers and sister had. Instead I was to go to the new, as yet, unknown teacher, Miss Berger, in room B-4. The A rooms were for the brighter students. Both A and B rooms were then further broken down into 3 classes; an A class for the brightest in the room, a B class for the in between students and a C class for the slowest students. It was such a disappointment and humiliation for me to go from Third Grade A room, Class A, to a Fourth Grade B room, Class C! However, at least I was passed.

But, things turned out fine. It was great after all, for Miss Berger was super; the best teacher ever. She was just what I needed after my third grade ordeals. Apparently she had just started teaching. This tall, slim, brown-eyed girl had long, dark hair that was pulled back into a soft knot at the nape of her neck. She always had a big, friendly smile for everyone. The entire class was won over very quickly, and even the "problem boys" caused no problems in her class.

One day, Miss Berger was out in the hall talking to another teacher (there were no teacher's meeting rooms in our school). Instead of waiting quietly or studying our assignments, we started talking and apparently talked and laughed too loudly. When she came back into the classroom, she told us how embarrassed and disappointed she was to have other classes and teachers hear *her class* behave that way. Miss Berger was near tears. We became very quiet, hanging our heads somewhat in shame, and it never, ever happened again - never, ever. The children would remind each other that we didn't want to hurt Miss Berger; that our class was much better than the A-4 class across the hall. And we acted like we were.

The school had a truant officer, a kindly, very old stoop shouldered gentlemen called Mr. Templeton. Every few days, he would make the rounds of all the classrooms to get the names of any absentee children. Few families had telephones in those days. If a child was absent for more than several days, Mr. Templeton went to their homes to see why they were not in school. He then would report this to the teacher on his next stop at that room.

Our class tried extra hard to have perfect attendance - we tried extra hard on everything to make

Miss Berger proud of us. If no one was absent when Mr. Templeton came to our classroom, Miss Berger had a special song we would sing to Mr. Templeton.

It went like this:

How do you do, Mr. Templeton?

How do you do?

We have 100% for you.

We will do it if we can

We will take it like a man

How do you do, Mr. Templeton?

How do you do?

We all stood up and sang the song with great pride, as loud as we could, so as to be heard all over the four grades of this "Baby Building." Especially, we wanted to show the other fourth grade how great our class was, even though we were supposed to be the B-4 room. I was so glad that I had contracted scarlet fever the year before, in the third grade, so that this year our class was able to get 100% so many more times.

Another song which we loved to sing came at Thanksgiving time. It was called the Big Fat Turkey song. Of course, we never had a turkey to eat at our house and no doubt many of my class mates had not either; but we sang this song loudly, accompanied by many arm and hand motions. It was a happy action song.

You would stand, clasping your hands, then spread out your arms making a large circle in front of you - and sing :

There's a big fat turkey down on Grandfather's farm, and he thinks he's very gay,
He spreads his tail
(hands now go straight up and slowly bringing the arms sideways down to shoulder level)
into a great big fan, and he struts around all day.
(everyone now struts or waddles about with arms outstretched)
You should hear him gobble at the girls and boys
(shaking a forefinger at the person next to you)
For he thinks he is singing when he makes that noise, But his song will be a different way -
(drawing a finger-knife across your throat)
skritch ! - upon Thanksgiving Day.

With Miss Berger's kindly encouragement, I soon progressed to her B and then A-class. After a time, I was on the honor roll again. Mother was often heard remarking to my Father that I was the first to go off to school in the morning and the last one to come home. Whenever possible, I was willing to stay after school to wash the boards, do extra class work or anything to be able to see more of Miss Berger.

Since Miss Berger was so loved by this class, we thought of what we might do that would be better than the other fourth grade did for their teacher. After all, our teacher was so much better and deserved more. Actually, I felt sorry for A-4 that they didn't have a teacher half as wonderful as Miss Berger. After much whispering on the school play ground (a solid brick play area to the front of the building), even though it was many weeks before Easter, we decided to start collecting money to buy our Miss Berger a nice, big, solid fruit and nut Easter egg.

Almost every few days, I asked Father for pennies or a nickel to add to the Easter egg money. He kept reminding me that he had already given me some a few days before. It seemed to take forever to convince him to let me have a bit more money. I told him that it was very important that we got enough money to buy a bigger egg than the other fourth grade was getting for their Miss Aubrey which would most likely be only a five pound egg.

Our class decided we should get Miss Berger a 10 pound egg, or at least a five pound egg and jelly beans and other chocolate figures. So, as hard as it was, I asked again and again for a few more pennies or another nickel from Father. Surely our entire class of over 40 children was doing the same, for we had collected far beyond our greatest expectations.

One boy's father had a car and at lunch time on the day before Easter vacation, he drove several classmates down to the local Candy Kitchen where all kinds of candies were made. We had raised so much money that we were able to buy not only an egg but other kinds of Easter candy as well.

Miss Aubrey kept our teacher busy in her room until we arranged our surprise on Miss Berger's desk. We covered the desk top with green Easter grass, small chocolate eggs, lots of jelly beans, chocolate rabbits of all sizes, other chocolate figures and marshmallow chicks. In the center of all this was a *great, big, beautiful* **25 pound** *egg*! We all thought it was the grandest display. How happy and satisfied we were with what we had done.

Follow up plans were discussed. Everyone agreed that Miss Berger was to have every bit of our Easter gift - **no one** was to take even one jelly bean. Without a doubt, such a wonderful teacher would invite us to have some of this Easter Feast of Feasts. Many times we reminded each other that we would not take any of the candy she might offer. Everyone agreed.

Can you imagine Miss Berger's surprise when she saw this! Of course she thanked us over and over. Try as she may though, there was *no way* she could convince any of us that we should have even a bit of it. How happy we were thinking we had given her the most and best thing imaginable - more than we even dreamed we could. Fortunately, we never thought about any problem she might have eating or distributing this lavish array - I hope she liked candy a lot and wasn't allergic to any of it.

I wonder what she did with all that candy. She only had a brother and they lived with their mother and father. We didn't think about that but I'm sure it was distributed well. Perhaps some was sent to an area orphanage.

Thinking about this now, it seems a bit foolish. Apparently no adult pointed out that we were going overboard with the candy thing; or if they did, we paid them no mind. We felt that if such a thing ever happened to any of us, it would be a dream come true. Today, these memories still make me feel happy and I'm glad a group of eight and nine year olds thought so much of a person to lavish all that on her. She was a teacher that treated everyone equally well and had no "teacher's pets," or we all felt like we each were. This was how she was able to win over any problem pupils and her class must have been a model class as well as a haven for those having a tough time of it.

The continuing depression brought more difficult times. . Many children could not afford to spend even a few pennies for the small bottle of milk that was offered mid-mornings each day at our public school. Over half of my class just watched as the other children drank milk at their desks. We pretended that we didn't care, nor want milk either. Of such a luxury I dared not dream.

One day, one of the "rich" children, who always got milk, was absent and the teacher handed me that bottle of milk! It was a heavenly, icy, cold nectar with wonderful rich cream on top. I do not remember ever having milk that tasted as good as this. Even though I sipped the milk very, very slowly , allowing this dream to last as long as possible, it was finished much too soon. I had been given a bit of the heaven some of the class enjoyed every morning at their desks.

The children drank the milk at their desks because our schools had no cafeteria or separate room for lunch - everybody went home for lunch each and every day. The teachers also went home and there was no one left in the school building with the possible exception of Mr. Williams, the janitor who stayed to re-stoke the coal furnace.

In our school, there wasn't even an office for the principal, Mr. Weaver. He taught third grade (B-3) and his classroom was also his office. Sometimes he used a paddle to discipline the boys, either in his classroom after school or in the hallway during school hours, where we could hear it all over the four grades of our "Baby Building". Paddling did not happen often but when it did, the sounds of the paddle smacking a boy's trousers and his cries reminded everyone to behave or possibly receive the same discipline.

Girls were spared from Mr. Weaver's paddling

or they must have behaved much better than the boys. I never knew of a girl that was paddled. The worst part of the punishment for the paddled boy was the teasing he got on his way home from school. Other boys, brave or foolhardy enough, would tease him with this song:

Johnny got a lickin',
Off of Mr. Weaver,

Jumped like a chicken,
Crowed like a rooster,

Cock-a-doo-del-doo!
(With wing flapping motions)

This song was repeated over and over until the tormented one either ran home faster or turned on his tormentors. Then there most likely would be another fight, with punching and rolling all over the ground, until a grownup pulled the boys apart and put an end to it. Without a doubt, this meant that there would be more patches on patches to mend someone's newly torn trousers.

Chapter VI

Mother and Father

Father had a most remarkable talent for language assimilation with a keen ear for regional accents and dialects. This was especially visible when he dealt with Greeks, Polish people and the special dialects of the Italian provinces. He could engage various customers in conversation, very easily laugh and joke with them. They would depart thinking that he had come from their own home town. Consequently he developed a clientele that extended widely into the country side. He found it profitable to buy a Ford truck, in addition to our big black Studebaker, so that he could deliver as well as take orders for home delivery.

During the ordinary week days of the year, business was such that Mother did not have to be in the store every minute and could attend to laundry, cooking, baking, or other house hold tasks. However, as the weekend approached, business would increase so that Mother was then required to be behind the counter constantly. She did the bookkeeping and attended to customers at those times when Father dealt with the traveling salesmen and delivery men from the wholesalers in Pittsburgh, Chicago and places in the East. This activity grew even more intense when church holidays and national holidays came on the scene.

Since Father could read very little, he managed his business and legal affairs with the help of my Mother and a close and trusted friend. Yet, he was probably one of the most intelligent persons I have ever known. Many people, even our doctor and local politicians, looked to him and took his advice on many matters. He had tons of common sense which helped us through many a problem. Mother, who was very well read for her era, made up for his lack of reading skills.

The first time Father saw Mother, she was sitting in a chair reading a book in the corner of her aunt's living room. She had arrived in this country from Aquara, Italy just the month before and was living with her aunt. She left her parents, sisters and brother in Italy to make herself a new life here in the States. Her older brother, who had already been here for several years, sent her the passage money so that she could join him in this country that was so good to him. Uncle Joe always told us she was his favorite sister. That, of course, made us very happy and we thought he was the greatest. During World War I, he had served his new country well in the U.S. Army and now held a very good job with the Pittsburgh Street Car Company.

It was the end of February in 1921 and another very cold winter. All winters seem very cold in Pennsylvania. Instead of letting his delivery man deliver, Father decided to make the delivery of groceries to the aunt's house himself.   Undoubtedly word got around about the arrival of this pretty young thing, my Mother.   He was quite smitten by this petite, young girl who sat apart from everyone, reading her book quietly in her aunt's living room.   She did not, or pretended not to, notice him.   He followed proper procedures and asked her brother for permission to call on Rosina.   Permission was granted to this very handsome and extremely successful businessman.

Mother, in talking to me about her courtship days, said that trays of cookies and freshly brewed coffee were made to enjoy at the aunt's home for this first meeting.   The aunt, Mother's brother Joseph, my Father (also named Joseph) and Mother enjoyed these refreshments while chatting and sitting around the dining room table.

At some point, Father then invited Mother to go to a movie with him.   She said she would, but only if her brother, her aunt, his mother, and his sister went, too!   Mother's aunt was embarrassed and horrified.   She poked Mother and exclaimed that "this is America and they don't do that here."   Mother replied, "I don't care.   If they don't go, I won't go."   Mother proudly told me that not only did Father take them all to the movies but he bought them ice cream afterwards!   That's how good and considerate   he was.   Apparently this was their only "date."   He told her he didn't have time for such things because of being so busy with the business of his store They were married shortly over a month later, on April. 5, 1921.

I would tease Mother and say that it wasn't that Father didn't have time to be "dating" her; it was more likely that he couldn't afford, and didn't want to take all those people out on a date each time.

This all came up when my older sister and I were to be married in a double wedding ceremony. For one thing, Mother couldn't understand this date - date - date thing, that the young people of our period carried on. We had been telling our parents of the wedding customs of the day - the mid 40's. The groom would pay for little more than his clothes, the rings, the license and clergy fees. The father of the bride paid for most everything else. The list was long. Father was to pay for everything else including our clothes, invitations, flowers at church, our flowers, the organist, wedding pictures, a brunch at a nearby restaurant, music and food for the reception to be held at the Polish Hall in town.

Mother told us that Father had paid for everything at their wedding: the license fees, a breakfast, wedding dinner with music, flowers, ceremony, photographs, rings and even for her wedding dress and shoes. And now was he expected to pay for his two daughters' weddings? But he did and it really wasn't very fair, I suppose.

Chapter VII

The Famous But True Zucchini Story

Today as I hear of the many people who say they do not like, cannot eat, or are allergic to various foods; I remember well my oldest sister, who one day at suppertime, suddenly insisted she could not eat zucchini for all these and other reasons.

It was the time of the Great Depression. The seven children in our family were just happy to have a good and filling meal which we relished without complaint. But there comes a time when one's garden produces zucchinis, more zucchinis, and more zucchinis till they seem to be taking over the world. Mother would prepare them day after day in various wonderful ways. They were stuffed with seasoned bread crumbs and rice, and then baked. They were battered and fried; or stewed with tomatoes and other vegetables fresh from the garden.

One evening she had sliced, seasoned and cooked them together with a bit of pork, chunks of hard old bread and grated Parmesan cheese. It was somewhat like a bread stuffing, - quite tasty, nourishing and filling.

This particular evening, Sister decided she would not eat zucchini anymore. She said she did not like zucchini because it made her sick and that she was allergic to it. This upset Mother quite a bit, for she saw the rest of us looking at our plates, wondering whether we should continue eating or follow my sister's lead. Father calmed Mother down by saying she should not worry about this and that he would take care of this problem later.

To help feed our large family and sell any surplus, Father had for some years rented a plot of ground, about an acre in size, for a vegetable garden. The farmer who owned the surrounding land would also plow our garden along with his many acres. This 'farm' of ours was four miles from town. The garden kept us busy during the summer time (our summer day camp?)! The hours we spent there meant that we would be too busy and too tired to get into any kind of mischief at home or in town.

Many a day I would walk to the garden and back with my brothers, two older and sometimes one younger than myself. When we walked, we would take the shortest route over gravel country roads with farm houses scattered here and there. The two youngest children and our oldest sister usually stayed at home with Mother. When we got to the garden, we four "farmers" would pull weeds, hoe corn, carry buckets of water from the creek to water plants, or do whatever we were asked to do. There was always time to climb trees, watch the ripples around the stones we dropped from the openings on the wooden bridge into the creek below, and swim and play in that creek that ran close to the garden.

About mid-day, Father would come to help and to bring a wonderful lunch. This we would eat in a shady gazebo that he and my brothers built in the middle of the field. Each year a new one was built. They chopped down small trees for the frame and thatched the roof with branches for shade.

At lunch time, someone would go to a nearby farmhouse for fresh milk and to the spring for cool, delicious water. For lunch there were always two long loaves of Italian bread, split down the middle. One loaf was buttered and generously layered with provolone, and at times with swiss or brick cheese. Some times fried sweet peppers would be added. The other loaf was layered with salami, cappicolo, proscuitto, etc. Sliced tomatoes and lettuce were added for good measure. For dessert, there was always fresh fruit. Such a feast!

A few days after the zucchini incident, Sis was told she was to help us for the day. This she did very grudgingly, especially since she did not look forward to the four mile walk out into the country. There was absolutely nothing to eat anywhere; neither fruit on the gnarled trees of the deserted orchard, nor berries on the prickly thorn bushes that lined the country road, and nothing yet ripe enough in the garden. There was no cupboard for crackers or cookies - absolutely nothing to chew on but the tender stems of the grass in the fields. It was the usual long, hard, hot morning's work, lightened only by the imagination and energy of lively children.

What a welcome sight to see Father's big black Studebaker come rolling down the dusty road about mid-day. We were famished. Lunch was later than usual; but eventually my two older brothers were sent across the covered, wooden bridge to the spring for glass gallon jugs of water to have with lunch. They were told not to get milk this time.

We settled down on hand hewn benches in the shade of the gazebo, starved for something to eat. With great deliberation, Father unwrapped one of the long loaves of bread and ceremoniously cut the loaf into enough pieces. He offered a piece to each of us; but when my sister saw that rather than the usual filling, it had fried zucchini and grated Parmesan cheese, she shook her head "No," and waited silently for the other loaf. We younger children devoured our pieces and were anxious for more. With a slight smile on his face, my father ate his piece quietly, relishing every mouthful while we waited and waited. It seemed forever before he was ready to cut the second loaf.

When   Father silently started to unwrap the second loaf, my sister jumped up to the table to get the first piece. But then, to her surprise and disappointment, this loaf was the same as the first, *filled with zucchini*. At first, she refused to eat the small piece offered to her, but then with a bit of urging from Father, she cautiously took a little nibble from the smallest piece, soon had quickly gobbled down the piece and then was asking for another.

That's all there was to it. Sister was cured of

her apparent inability to eat zucchini and she never ever acted so obstinately at the table again. In fact, after she married, zucchini was a favorite dish of her dinner menus. She served it so often, in so many wonderful ways, you would think she invented zucchini!

Chapter VIII

Days of Regret

Long beautiful hair has been said to be a girl's crowning glory. To me, long and braided hair was nothing but a pain and a problem, especially when trying to get to school in the morning. Mother would comb and braid my hair, in between doing the many other things necessary to get four children off to school on time. More than several times, when the comb would pull a knot in my hair or catch the small looped gold earrings in my ears, I would squirm and say "ouch". As soon as I was grown enough I did without those earrings and I have not worn pierced earrings since.

Father would only cut the boys' hair, refusing to cut the girls' hair. After all, long hair was feminine, and his girls were not going to have short hair. So it was that one day I took the matter into my own hands. I took Father's hair cutting scissors and started to do the job myself. Part of my braids were already cut off when I was found out. There was nothing else to be done now but for Father to salvage the job I had bungled.

The resulting style was more drastic than I thought it would be. My brothers teased me, saying that now since I looked like a boy that I would become a boy. No! I did not want to look like nor to be a boy! My parents tried to assure me this would not be so; but how could I take a chance?

I ran upstairs to the bathroom, crying, and put my head under running water, as my brother suggested, to make it grow. Through heavy tears I checked myself in the mirror many times, but I could see no change. Eventually, the tears stopped . Reality overtook me and I resigned myself to wait for a more girlish hairdo.

When one is young, time goes on forever, and each day seems to be like the day before. Nothing new marks those days and they slip into the dimness of last week.

Then there came one of those summer days that smelled of adventure and excitement, when everything is keyed to a high pitch and one was willing to risk much to escape boredom.

Another brother and I were invited to join our oldest sister and brother upstairs to see something secret. They had somehow managed to get one of the four inch Italian stogies. They brought the cigar up to one of the bedrooms. There, with whispers of conspiracy and threatening words of caution, they lit up the stogie with great showmanship.

At first, the younger brother and I just watched as they demonstrated to us how expertly they could smoke. Since smoking didn't seem difficult for them, I suspect they had done this before and were just trying to impress us now. They carefully blew the smoke out of a wide open window so that our parents would not smell the foul smoke, for then they certainly would discipline us soundly.

I was fascinated by the way they could make smoke come out of their mouths. Eventually, after the three had their fill of this wicked thrill, the cigar was passed on to me. All three impatiently gave me instructions on how to smoke. I found it easy enough to puff the smoke in, but impossible to get the smoke to come back out of my mouth. Naturally, I swallowed a lot of some very potent stuff, and it seemed that I never would get the hang of it.

As their consciences started to kick in, they all became excitedly nervous and said I should give up before we got caught. But, I persisted. Eventually, I was smoking and was blowing just as much smoke out the window as the three of them had been doing. Suddenly, the most awful sickening feeling came over me. Somehow, I summoned the strength to throw that cigar across the yard onto the slanted roof of our warehouse next door. It rolled down onto the ground below and my brother hurriedly ran down to retrieve and quietly dispose of the burning cigar.

Oh, was I sick! Instead of dying, I crawled over to my bed and remained there for the longest time, recovering and regretting this terrible thing I had done to myself. No one could call Mother to help me, for we would be found out and reap the dire consequences.

Still, I now believe our parents must have known what was going on in that upstairs bedroom. Sometimes I wonder if the cigar wasn't deliberately put out by them, so that we would have this awful experience at an early age and never smoke again. It most likely was not just coincidence that the next day my Mother asked me, only me, if I knew how to smoke. I answered that I did. She asked me to show her and I said I didn't want to, but repeated several times that I really knew how to smoke. Just the thought of smoking made me ill. Mother smiled knowingly and the subject was never brought up again; proving that she truly must have had eyes in the back of her head, and ears that heard everything, no matter where we were.

From that time on, the smell of any cigarette, cigar or pipe smoke made me feel ill. Sometimes when I was the only non-smoker in an office or at a restaurant dining table and some smoker lit up, it totally destroyed my composure and appetite.

That was tough to bear. I was forced to silently endure this foul atmosphere that permeated my clothing and even the hair on my head. Today's non-smoking attitude is very much appreciated. I still feel sorry for smokers so addicted to tobacco. I am glad my smoking career began and ended the same day; before I "grew up".

On another summer day, when our yard was filled with children, their activity had covered it all with scattered newspapers. Mother came out and directed us to pick up every scrap. As we proceeded, I thought of a faster way and, using a pitch fork, began stabbing about, picking up all these pieces. As I approached my sister who was just standing there, I asked her to move so I could pick up the piece under her foot. But she continued to talk away, ignoring me, and I felt she would move her foot as I got closer. To our mutual surprise, I kept stabbing on; she didn't move and I stuck the fork into her foot. She screamed; I ran to Clay Hill several blocks away in an attempt to escape home and certain punishment.

I stayed several hours there, regretting my rash action, and wondering how I would survive, drinking rain water and eating the weeds in the fields. I wished the day could start over and that the afternoon could have been without incident.

My brothers eventually found me, and assured me that while the accident was not understood by my parents, the punishment I imagined awaited me on my return would not be given. But in my fright I did not believe them, for I had done such a terrible thing and was deserving of any disciplinary action they could think of.

As night drew near I knew I had to face the music. Accompanied by my brother, I returned home. There my parents told me I now had to take on all of my sister's chores as well as my own for weeks to come. While my sister now sat in her chair with her bandaged foot propped up, quite content with her lot, I washed and dried the dishes, doing all her tasks, happy that I wasn't skinned alive.

Chapter IX

Pasta, Parmesan e Baccala

For Christmas Eve supper, our traditional menu for the children would include Angel Hair pasta served to them with butter, chopped parsley, and grated Parmesan cheese. The adults were served their Angel Hair pasta with an anchovy sauce. Prepared with hot olive oil; softly cooked minced garlic, parsley, some mashed anchovies, and a little added water; it was quickly poured over a heated platter of prepared pasta. Garnished with anchovy fillets, and more parsley; this pasta course was served with grated Parmesan, Romano or Pecorino cheese.

We had a rule for determining whether to make a thick or thin sauce for the various pasta dishes we enjoyed. The rule was: if you were having a large pasta like rigatoni or lasagna, a thicker sauce was made using both tomatoes and tomato paste, relying more on the flavor of the tomato. For the thin pastas like spaghettini and linguini, a lighter tomato sauce was made, usually without the tomato paste. This allowed the flavors of the meats and spices to come through, rather than being smothered up by the tomato paste. Sometimes the Capellinis and Angel Hair pastas were served only in a rich, clear broth; always very good, always a treat.

Outside our store, among other Christmas

items, were whitened wooden cages holding cackling hens and quacking ducks. Roosters would crow throughout all the hours of the day; waking us in the early morning and reminding the hens of their particular jobs. The poultry were, for the most part, a weekend item. It was almost unheard of to buy poultry that you did not see alive and healthy. No one seemed to want poultry that was dressed and lying cold in a cooler in some store. Customers liked to see their choice as healthy-looking spry chickens.

Families bought live poultry then. Father would reach into a cage and, finding the particular hen selected by the customer, grab the squawking bird by the legs and drag it out. He would place it, one hand still grasping its feet, on the spring balance nearby. If the weight suited the customer, Father swept the bird into the store, flopped it down on some paper on the counter, and tied its feet with twine. He then shoved it into a brown paper bag with one hole torn out in the bottom so that the hen's head would poke through, allowing the bird to protest its loss of dignity while the customer carried it home. Some people preferred not having it wrapped, but simply carried the bird home by its feet, upside down, for all to admire.

At home, it wasn't always the man of the house who disposed of the bird's life by wringing its neck or chopping off the head and leaving it to bleed as it flopped around. But it was usually left to the women to scald, pluck and otherwise prepare the hen or duck for cooking. Geese were items all to themselves, as their plucking provided an extra bonus, that of fluffy goose feathers and down for the making of pillows and bed comforters Turkeys were rare birds to have, for they were not yet as popular an item as they are today. We saw very few of them.

I do not remember Father or Mother preparing poultry for anyone except for our own use. Frequently it would be my task to scald and pluck several hens at a time for our Sunday dinner. After all the feathers were removed, the bird was passed over a gas flame on the stove to burn off any hairs left on the bird. The heart, liver, gizzard and giblets were removed and cleaned properly. The entrails were disposed of in various ways.

Carefully, the bile duct was removed from the liver, so that it would not burst and contaminate whatever it touched with its bitterness. The liver and heart were sautéed as special treats for my father and brothers, as were any eggs not yet laid.

The gizzard was cut open to remove the sack membrane that held corn, chicken feed not yet digested, and perhaps a few stones. The gizzard together with the wings, neck, feet and back were put in a kettle of cold water and brought to a slow simmer. The foamy scum was skimmed off the surface a number of times with a tablespoon; until no more scum could be seen.

Our parents told us the foamy scum that came to the top of the soup broth was not healthy for us. If the scum were not removed, later in life we would have problems with the joints of our bones - the substance would act like a cement. It could even clog the drain of the kitchen sink. So scum was always put into the garbage. Religiously, carefully and completely removing the foamy scum was something I *always* did (even after I married and still to this day). True or untrue - I don't know for certain if the foamy soup scum would cause health problems, but I do know that the people of our family did not have aching bones and neither I nor they suffer from arthritis.

To the now clear broth were added several large onions, quartered a bit more than half way so they wouldn't come apart in cooking. A good bit of celery leaves came next, some cut up celery stalks, whole canned tomatoes (usually the plum) and perhaps a few carrots, followed by parsley when it was available. This was cooked for quite some time. Just before serving, salt and pepper were tastefully added. Since chicken feet are not easily available today, one cannot duplicate the gelatinous richness of this broth.

We enjoyed this broth, the likes of which you cannot believe. It was a rather clear broth that was lightly colored by the tomatoes and with a delicate, delicious taste of the other seasonings and rich poultry flavors blended together. It was so comforting to have a cup of this broth, perhaps with some oyster crackers or some hard, dry, Italian bread. Other times, a portion of the large broth pot was added to one of the many pastinas, cooked al dente, just a few minutes before serving. This dish, topped with grated cheese, was one of everyone's favorites.

From time to time we were reminded by Father to be aware of the health benefits that proper foods gave us. He emphasized that it was best to eat a well rounded array of foods in order to have good and strong bodies. He likened it to the building of a house. "You cannot build a strong house using just sand and perhaps one or two other materials," he would say. "So it is with your bodies, you must eat many fruits and vegetables along with meat and other foods. Sweets should be used very little. Then you will hardly ever need medicines or laxatives and all these other things people are taking."

" *La, la, la* - - *Pesche Stocka e Baccala*" - this is what my parents sang in the fall when all the fish started to arrive from Gorton's Seafood Company of Boston, Massachusetts. The various fishes provided us wonderful meals which we could never have at any other time of the year, partly because of a lack of re-frigeration. Some of the fish I recall were: sword-fish, smelts, clams, baccala or codfish (both fresh and dried,) whole dried stock fish, eels or capitone, shrimp, calimari, whiting, squid, salmon, haddock and halibut. There might even be octopus, shark and tuna.

Dried codfish (baccala) was soaked overnight in water which was changed several times to remove much of the salt used to preserve it. This made it as flaky as fresh cod but with a distinctive flavor we all enjoyed in a salad, in a stew with tomatoes, or floured and fried.

For Christmas Eve, the refreshed cod was cooked and the bones removed. It was then flaked, mixed and tossed with a goodly amount of celery leaves, a little salt and lots of freshly ground black pepper, olive oil and several cut cloves of garlic. Served in a large bowl, this became another salad for our holiday table on Christmas Eve. It was traditional to have seven different kinds of fish for Christmas Eve supper in reflection of the seven holy sacraments. We certainly had seven types and more.

There would be boiled and shelled shrimp; tuna or steak fish (shark), floured and fried smelts; pickled herring; squid pouches stuffed with rice, seasonings and grated cheese; clams; calamari; cod, fried and in salad; plus anchovies in a garlic olive oil sauce for the angel hair pasta. Two pasta bowls laced with good, freshly grated Parmesan cheese and fresh green parsley would be a central focus of the table.

Finocchio, crisp, green, feathery-topped, anis-flavored Italian celery, along with regular celery, would be placed on platters with small dishes of olive oil blended with lots of pepper and salt for dipping. We called finocchio Christmas celery, because in those days this treat would only be seen at that time of year. Today it is in the produce departments of grocery stores almost year-round.

Thick slices of wonderful bread were always there for dipping or to accompany the good food along with a very generous green salad made with escarole, endive, lettuce, and black olives. On another platter a wreath of broccoli, interlaced with pimento, added to the sumptuous array. Dishes and trays of dried figs (some stuffed with nuts), plump dates, roasted or boiled chestnuts, nuts of all kinds, little sweets, and fresh fruits would complete our Christmas Eve feast.

Chapter X

The Seasons

The many deliveries that came to our store during the holiday season brought lots of extra things to sell. Then the store became a bit like the earlier, lively, bustling prosperous years before the Depression. We loved tasting the treats of torrone, an almond-nougat candy, wrapped in silver paper and put in beautiful little boxes with pictures of historic Italian figures. My favorite confection was the flat six inch rounds of wonderful hazel nut and citrus paneforte. There were the crisp almond flavored amorettas, all sorts of the best biscotti you ever tasted, and many more cheeses and specialty meats than we had all year. For grown ups, there were various sized bottles of sweet and dry vermouths, amorettas, anisette and other liqueurs.

Besides the creamy ricotta cheese that I still love, there was a special and favorite cheese which we children called "Baby Doll Cheese." It was really a type of Scamorze cheese, with a small ball of butter already in it. It was shaped like a little fat five inch or so golden yellow pouch and pinched at the top leaving a flower-like ruffle. When it was sliced, you found a golden ball of sweet, creamy butter in the middle.

It's still a mystery to me how this cheese with a butter center was made. How convenient - you could have cheese and butter for your bread all in one container. And, it was umm - so good. I have not seen or heard of this cheese for many, many years. I wonder if someone still makes it. If so, today it would undoubtedly cost a fortune. Wouldn't it be great to take a pouch of this cheese on a picnic with a good friend, some bread, fruit and a cold drink?

In the spring season the store would be surrounded with bedding plants of all types: tomatoes; cabbages; peppers - the sweet, the green, the long and yellow and very hot Hungarian; egg plant; celery; broccoli; cauliflower; varieties of annual flowers; as well as parsley; sweet basil; rosemary; thyme and other herbs. So much was stored in our building next door as well as up and down the yard in between the buildings, it sometimes became difficult to walk on the little bit of a path that was left. Seed stands would be prominently displayed about the store, as would all sizes of clay pots, filled with colorful annuals.

Summer brought large amounts of green vegetables raised on our own country acre that was four miles from town, as well as the local farms or from the farms of southern states and California. Father would rise early in the morning and drive about an hour away to the Market on the strip in Pittsburgh where the railroads came in. He would buy whatever he needed or wanted from the wholesalers there. By eight o'clock he would be home, cleaning his purchases, and preparing his window displays.

Father would bring back melons of every type, mostly Georgia grown. Bananas on the stalk, were hung in the display window. Oranges, lemons, limes, July apples, red tomatoes, purple eggplant, okra, fennel, artichokes, celery, strawberries, cherries from California, corn from Florida and vegetables of all kinds he would display in the window. His supply of cheeses, olives and other such items would be replenished as needed if they were not to be delivered from special wholesalers.

In those days refrigeration in the home was obtained from 25 pound blocks of ice. These blocks were delivered on ice trucks from a local ice house and placed in your "ice box", which was the forerunner of the electrical refrigerator. The "Monitor" by GE and the "Frigidaire" had not yet come on the market. Mechanical refrigeration was enjoyed only by the wealthy. Much larger blocks were used in the store "ice box." Eventually, we did get a refrigerated display case for the meats and cheeses but still kept the big "ice box" for milk and fresh meats.

On steamy summer days, Father would bring out a large metal tub with a lid. He would fill it with chopped ice and stock it with flavored pop and soda from the local Nehi bottler and with Vernor's ginger beer and ginger ales. He might also snuggle in a few melons. Later on, in the almost unbearably humid heat of the day, he would sell long thick melon slices, cut the full length of the melon, calling out this ditty with his wonderful voice:

> *Watermelon, watermelon, five cents a slice*
> *Ice cold watermelon, five cents a slice.*
>
> *Five cents.*
> *Five cents.*
> *Five cents a slice.*
>
> *Eat, drink, and wash your face for five cents a slice.*
> *Ice cold watermelon, five cents a slice.*

The people would love it, quickly buying all the melon he had cut and enjoying it right there where they stood on the sidewalk in front of the store.

Father never forgot the national holidays. He would fly the flag at the front of the store on every occasion. Mother would not let him sell fireworks on the Fourth of July, but we all loved to stand outside and watch the fantastic, long parades as they went by. The whole town would come out to see the parades. If you weren't in it, you sat on the curb to watch these yearly events, while the grown ups brought out chairs to sit on, to see the parade and to watch over us.

Dozens of marching bands from our neighboring towns would come , as well as a like number of fire trucks, some with one or two of their crew dressed as clowns. There were the usual red trucks as well as a few white and yellow trucks. The trucks clanged their big bells and sounded their sirens, while the firemen waved to the crowds and peppered them with candy. Of course, there were the many cars and sleek convertibles with the Mayor, other politicians, the Chief of Police and other "who knows who" types.

There were also the horse back riders, motor cyclists, Boy Scouts and Girl Scouts in uniform, marching along with the veterans of several wars and more. It was something not to be missed. I believe almost all the homes were empty. Those townspeople not in the parade were now solidly lining the parade route. The parades of that period were big productions compared to many of today's parades with few bands and many trucks and cars advertising this or that.

As fall drew near, Father would have canning supplies on hand to sell to al most all the homemakers, who canned much of the harvests produced for later use at their dining tables. Ball glass jars and zinc lids, jar rubbers, seasonings of all kinds, dill for pickling, sugar by the twenty five pound bag, lard by the five gallon can, flour in the big 25 pound cloth sacks (that later could be sewn into dresses and under garments), root beer extract, bottle caps, bottling machines and sealing wax helped preserve the harvest.

There were so many things, such as cabbage shredders to make sauerkraut, pasta makers, tomato machines to press the juices from tomatoes for canning, crocks of all sizes; it hurts my mind to think of them all. There would be heaps of pumpkins, pears, grapes, apples, plums, the list goes on. There would be pies to make, as well as compotes, jellies, apple butter, and other arts of the home maker, nearly forgotten today. We would make pickles, canned peaches, canned tomatoes - as a juice, sauce, chopped, whole and pureed. We even made a bit of ketchup.

As Thanksgiving Day approached, my Father usually would have a live turkey among the poultry cages and he would become more relaxed and in tune with the calendar because the following day, the Christmas season was beginning. The elders of our youth became concerned when the commercial side of this season started any earlier. As we grew up we saw the commercial side of Christmas appear after Halloween, and recently we have seen it appear before Labor Day, as proprietors seek to be first in the market.

Chapter XI

The Dark Age

The Depression changed what had been a comfortable life for our family, which had grown to include seven children of whom I was the middle child. Our town was a small borough in rolling farm country which had underneath it large coal deposits. It had the railroads which carried out the coal, so that brought in some steel working industry. There also was a working uranium deposit being mined for the clays that would give a beautiful color to chinaware because of the uranium it contained. But the national economy died, and with it our town began to wither. Stores and mills closed for lack of business, and many people lost their livelihood for an unbelievably long period of time.

Companies, that did not close down completely, pushed for more production from fewer workers, without implementing newer methods and machines. Trouble arose. The coal mines seemed to be under the greatest stress. Too many times, too many miners were trapped and died in the underground shafts. Workers, especially coal miners, went on strike (most of all for safer working conditions) asking only pennies more in higher wages and shorter working hours. Labor strife entered our community with such a vengeance that work slowed almost to a stand still.

We all know the sad song that must have been about these miners and this era:

"Sixteen tons and what do you get,
Another day older and deeper in debt,

—

I owe my soul to the company store."

It seems the miners were required to work very long hours in dangerous underground mines. They were forced to shop at company owned stores, where the prices were much higher. Since their low wages were paid in scrip, redeemable only at these stores, families were kept in debt much of their lives, almost in bondage.

Company police from the coal mine corporation roamed the town at will, riding through on horseback, accompanied by their big, vicious-looking dogs. The local authorities did not dare to interfere with their actions. If the coal miners tried to hold meetings to organize a union or whatever, these police would have their horses rear up to break the meeting room windows with their hooves. They would send in their snarling dogs to disperse the meeting. The Company Police were known to drag men from their homes, and beat up the leaders of these meetings.

My brothers would run home excitedly saying that the Company Police were going to so and so's home. I would run indoors to hide from all this, but I remember seeing them go by a number of times. Ever since I have had a fear of dogs. How glad I was that my Father was not a coal miner.

Meanwhile, the depression continued on forever, or so it seemed. Father let credit be extended far too long before he put an end to it, requiring cash payments only. The paralysis of business in general, and the drying up of cash income to our store, brought the specter of doom even to the threshold of our family.

Father had a harder and harder time meeting his tax obligations. The savings my parents had accumulated since the store opened in 1921 were soon completely depleted. The ever-present threat of losing, not only the store but our own home, resulted in a daily nightmare for all of us. We children couldn't help but know in part what was going on.

My Father practically kept the whole town fed for the longest time. And later, when he refused to give any more credit, Mother would intercede and ask him to let this and that particular family have up to a certain amount more credit, to insure their children had something to eat and at least have soap to wash with.

Unfortunately, even though some returned to work, few repaid their debts to Father. There were a few families whom my parents never dreamed would ever pay their debt; however they did pay every cent; a bit now and more another time.

Some, who could have paid their debts off easily, required my father to come week after week for only a coin or two towards their huge bill. Excuses they gave a-plenty. We watched as families, who had built up large bills with us even scold Father. "What will the neighbors say when they see you coming week after week?" How demoralizing for him and for us all.

These people in my view, were out and out robbers, stealing from us in this awful way. They were unappreciative and quickly forgot that their families had been able to eat and stay alive because of the credit and goodness extended toward them. But, perhaps it is their guaranteed ticket to hell; the bigger the debt, the deeper into the bowels of hell they may go. Certainly the same happens today and it is far worse when it happens within families.

Some repaid *nothing* at all. They went instead to the newly opened cash and carry supermarket, where though the prices were pennies lower, they were always required to pay cash for their purchases. They spent money on tap dancing classes, trips, and such for their children and themselves. How could anybody forget that they owed so much money and keep making excuses for not paying yet spending on what were truly luxuries?

One summer day the local deputy posted Sheriff's Sale signs on all the properties on our street. Father was out in the country working in the garden with my brothers. Mother became hysterical when she saw the sign being posted on the telephone pole in front of our store. She cried out that we had worked and worked to pay our taxes for years. We were doing all that could be done. Yet now, without compassion, we were to be "thrown out into the street like dogs!"

Since I happened to be at home, Mother gave me a dime to take the streetcar which would more quickly get me fairly close to Father. I had never yet taken the streetcar alone anywhere. My parents hardly let me go to the corner alone. I couldn't have been more than about seven. Yet now, in hysterical desperation, Mother was pleading with me to deliver this awful news to Father and fast! The sheriff's sale was only weeks away!

I clutched the dime in my fist and started running. Rather than taking the shorter dirt country road, I went the longer highway route to the garden, for the streetcar had just passed our house. Perhaps I would catch another one at a halfway stop about two miles from home. Besides, we would need *every* penny to save our property from that awful sheriff and it might not cost a whole dime to ride the streetcar from that stop.

When my sides began to ache sharply, I still kept on running but more slowly. Soon I could continue only by walking. When I saw the street car coming at that halfway point, I gave up my money and rode it to the Crossroads' stop.. The ride did my aching sides good. I jumped off the streetcar, ran the rest of the distance down the highway to the dirt road that led to the garden.

My brothers saw me running across the covered wooden bridge and called to Father. He put down his hoe and came running to me. After I sobbed the news to him, he put me in the Studebaker to ride home immediately. He told the boys they were to continue working and walk home when they were finished.

Our parents never gave up. Every pebble was turned. They went to a well-to-do-friend who refused to help. We later learned that this man wanted to buy up the entire block for himself. His greed did not care about Father's plight, nor the families and the many children that were to be displaced. Since Father owned the two largest lots in the middle of this area and would not sell, the "friend" was foiled and could not proceed. with his plan.

What days of torment and tears everywhere on our block. How helpless everyone felt. There seemed to be nowhere for us to turn for help. The government was a faceless monster interested only in gathering tax money. The banks would only lend you money if you didn't need it. The church would only pray for you. It would not even help find someone to give bodily and physical sustenance. A letter to the President of the United States did absolutely no good. It seemed that every body turned their backs on those in the grip of this catastrophe.

The government had a relief program to help people who were out of work. For businesses facing devastation, it seems they could have done more good by extending a helping hand. Our neighborhood's businesses were owned by good, proud, hard working people who always paid their taxes when they were able. If they had been allowed to stay and struggle through until the economy improved, a more humanitarian government could have profited in the long run. Instead, they supported the senseless destruction of this neighborhood.

As I lay awake at night I pictured that awful sheriff "throwing us out into the street like dogs". Well, I made plans to fool him and run out into the street before he could even touch me.

All our friends were forced to move. Most moved in with relatives in other states. Our Greek neighbors, the John's, moved from the home behind their Coffee House on our street, to a small upstairs apartment at the other end of town.

For a time, the John children refused to go to the school closer to their new home. Instead they walked in all kinds of weather a very long distance to our school. They had no rain gear or umbrellas. We encouraged them to keep coming. They packed lunches and ate with us in our home. But winter was approaching and there surely would be snowfalls that would reach the youngest child's shoulders. They were forced to give up even more of their pride and go to the school closer to their home. I was too young to go very far from home, so I never saw or heard from them again. Hopefully, all these neighbors came through this nightmare and are living good and healthy lives.

Finally, our parents did overcome this ordeal. Our Godparents had another small house which was now rented out. It was the first house they ever owned. Selling it for very little cash was quite a sacrifice to their family. This money was loaned to us but it paid only for part of the tax money the Sheriff required. Mr. Light, our insurance agent, found a farmer from his church who loaned us the rest of the money. Mother's ceaseless tears and painful cries now turned to joy. Of course, that awful sheriff never got to throw anyone of our family "out into the street like dogs."

Father could have declared bankruptcy but never would do so. He took pride in taking care of his personal responsibilities. He paid his bills and we did with very, very little for many years, never truly recovering from that period. Our parents looked upon debt as something evil and we were cautioned to pay cash or do without.

Chapter XII

A Light at the End of the Tunnel

Our parents, in addition to repaying the debt to our Godparents and the kind farmer, continued to pay on the orders they had placed with the wholesale grocery companies while waiting for payment from the credit customers.

At the dinner table, there wasn't much conversation. But sometimes my parents would talk of ways they might be able to struggle through this difficult period. As a small child, I remember overhearing them discussing the troubling events of the day; how this and that family was having a tough time. I wondered how anyone could be much worse off than we were. Many families were getting help from government relief programs. My parents were too proud to even dream of taking one cent of charity. We had what we had and we would have to wait, doing what we could until better fortune came to us, whenever that might be.

One day before Thanksgiving, when Father was not at home, the Salvation Army delivered to our house the bushel basket of food they were distributing to all poor families. How hurt Father was when he returned and saw this. Apparently someone, seeing my brother's much patched trousers and our meager clothing, put our family on the list to receive this charity. Father had the basket taken to the basement immediately and planned to return it. The dressed chicken, he scoffed at, saying it most likely had been a *sick* chicken before it had been butchered; not really fresh, so not fit to eat.

We, children, spotted a box of Jello in the bushel basket and, somehow, managed to talk Father into letting us keep it. Jello was something we no longer carried in the meager inventory of our store. This charitable offering never came again. Father must have let the proper people know not to send charity groceries to our grocery store again.

A few weeks before school started, my Father would often load up his Ford truck in the early morning with groceries and go far into the country, farm to farm to sell these groceries to make money for our school clothes. He went more often during this period. The feelings I had when he did this were very unsettling, for his truck by then was old and not always dependable. I worried about the long hours he was gone, to heaven only knows where.

How my Mother worried when he did not get back until long after dark; for with its problems, the truck broke down too often. I watched her worry, felt her pain and worried, too. I pictured all sorts of awful things happening to my Father. Could there have been an accident? Did someone rob my Father or beat him up? Or perhaps he had a flat tire and was alone in the dark with no one to help him. What a mountain of work he took on for his family. It was a great relief to hear that truck come clanking home.

The money Father made was used to buy one new dress for my older sister and one for me to be worn on the first day of school. The Depression was brutal as I entered first grade. For years, I remember having one new and one other rather old dress to use for school, rarely anything more.

There was no closet in my bedroom. This bedroom was one that I shared with my sister until she went away to work (couldn't afford to go to college). But we did have a nifty place to hang our dresses. About half way up on one wall of our bedroom there was a small gas pipe about 8" long sticking out of the wall. It was at the just right height for us to reach.

Made of ornamental brass twisted in a spiral shape, the pipe was an art form we turned to practical use. The end of the pipe once had a gas mantel; all that remained now was a little jet where we could ignite a yellow flame for light if the power went off. A flat thumb sized knob let us turn the gas on or off. As this was no longer used, we put our dresses on wooden hangers and hooked them over this dandy outlet. There was room to hang many more dresses, if we had them.

Hoping to make it appear that we had more than two dresses, one dress would be worn Monday and Tuesday; then we would wash it by hand. The other dress was worn Wednesday and Thursday, then washed. Of course the Monday and Tuesday dress was worn again on Friday.

Today I am certain that everyone must have known how poor we were and that we really just had two dresses, but we felt better about spreading the two dresses out over the week like this. The floors of our rooms were not cluttered as many of today's children's are, for we had few clothes, toys or possessions to clutter our room with.

You must know that these dresses were not the wash and wear ones of today either. Almost every night (or early morning) my sister and I would be ironing our own dress for school. It was also necessary that we wash our long white cotton stockings and underwear nightly, because we had only a pair or two.

Hardly ever would my brothers get a new pair of trousers or perhaps a shirt to begin school. At times, they wore trousers with patches over patches. And that was the best to be done about it.

It was more difficult to determine who got new shoes. That depended on who's shoes were shabbiest, or who had the most worn-out pair, or who had considerably outgrown theirs. We could no longer afford to take our shoes to the shoe repair shop in town.

Father learned to repair our shoes himself. With the many pairs of shoes needing repairs about our home, he did this often. He had a tall metal stand that accepted interchangeable metal shoe forms of different sizes corresponding to the size shoe needing repair. With a special knife, a sole was cut from a slab of leather to fit the shoe and then nailed in place. Heels were bought and nailed down. Shoes used to be sold in our store, but no longer. That part of the stock had to be discontinued. Fortunately books, pencils and tablets were furnished by the schools.

Despite the lack of very much money, people still had to eat and would save to afford even more during the busy holiday season. Then our parents, without the outside help they could no longer afford, would work about 18 hours a day, often seven days a week. The seven children of our family helped with whatever chores they were given. Besides the every day household tasks of food preparation and cleanup; each of us, but especially the boys, was required to help with all the store work connected with the selling of the usual groceries and the extra merchandise of the holiday season as well.

We washed the windows, swept the sidewalk, stocked the shelves, restacked the canned goods displays, took out the refuse generated by cleaning vegetables, swept up and put down fresh, clean sawdust. We learned to work at an early age for our own good and the welfare of the family.

In some fashion, we replaced the outside help. In those days, it was unheard of to get any sort of allowance for tasks that had to be done. We simply took pride and satisfaction from doing our chores. Then again, if we didn't do our chores, we risked punishment from our parents. Only many years later did we hear of the word allowance; but by then we were earning money of our own and also giving a part of our earnings back to the family, until we married.

A major portion of the money that I earned, after graduating from high school, went to the family
monthly. A smaller portion I put aside to pay for
things required for work, such as my clothes, trans-
portation (street car fare), lunch money, and personal
health. There were no medical plans then. Dental
care, and surgical treatments had to be prepared and
saved for. Through prudent savings I even managed
to buy my parents a set of living room furniture,
which was on sale at Kaufman's Dept. Store, in Pittsburgh.

The period several weeks before Christmas was
when my parents worked the hardest and longest,
selling fresh seafood. Every few days deliveries arrived all the way from Gorton's Fish Company in
Boston. Everything was well packed with lots of ice.
These boxes and large wooden crates were set outside in front of the store where they were readily seen
and stayed cold in our freezing Pennsylvania winters.
It seemed cruel to have to go out in brutally cold
weather and handle the cold, cold seafood amid all
that ice. But, our parents did this and all they could
to get us through the Depression alive.

One might think we as children were fairly
well off, since Father still had this store, even though
it now was a thin shadow of its former self. Other
children who had grown up in poverty have told me
that they never knew they were poor or deprived.
Well, we once had seen a filled store that served
many people. Now inventory was kept at a mini-

mum, and sales were small. Maintaining the store required all of Father's ready cash, so that little money remained for our own use. There was hardly anything left for clothing. There was no money at all for toys, bicycles or roller skates, no magazines or books for general reading, and no medical or dental care, or other emergency medical attention. We did always have something to eat, but more often it would be those things that did not sell and whatever we grew ourselves. My cupboards today hold almost as much as the stock that was left on the shelves of this once great store.

Many of the bright lights were turned off. Some were replaced with lower wattage bulbs. As little heat as possible was used to save as much money as could be saved. Our store was reduced to a rather sad and depressing place. What a heartbreak it must have been for our parents. To save even more, yet keeping us fed, Mother started to bake bread for our use rather than take the bread brought in on the bakery truck. At ten cents a loaf, the bakery bread was more expensive than home made bread. And our family ate a lot of bread. The many long hours of the once thriving business were no more. Now there was more time and less money. When there was any bakery bread left over several days after delivery, we might have the hard bread to dip into our breakfast hot milk laced with coffee. That was our complete breakfast, no butter or jelly either. On very rare occasions, like a holiday, we might have eggs and such.

To make our own bread, Mother would put 25 pounds of flour at one time, into the biggest pan you can imagine and made a dough that was used for a number of things besides bread. It was quite an exhausting chore for this little five foot mother of mine to properly mix and knead all that dough. After it had raised, most of the dough would be formed into round and long loaves of various sizes. Some dough would be pinched off, rolled into sticks, then twisted and braided into larger loaves. These we called "baby dolls". More dough was pulled into four inch strips, fried like donuts, sugared and enjoyed as a special treat. For our meal that day several large pizzas, topped with a fresh tomato sauce, would be made from part of the remaining dough.

Our big black stove had two ovens to bake the bread. One oven was a gas oven and the other was heated with a wood fire. The breads came out of the ovens looking like those shown in today's gourmet magazines. We begged to have some hot bread, but we were told hot bread would give us a stomach ache. It must have been that our parents knew that we would eat too much of the delicious hot bread too quickly. They wanted the bread to last our family of nine for a week, at least.

The delightful aroma of bread as it baked would fill not only our house but the whole neighborhood. Surely, this is what heaven will smell like - nothing else but fresh baking bread.

Chapter XIII

Our Very Own Tree

Today it is difficult to imagine anyone celebrating the Christmas season without some sort of a tree, whether it is an evergreen or one of the thousands of other choices, from the simple plastic to the elaborate artificial types used. I was almost six years old before our family put up our first evergreen tree, on Christmas Eve.

Before that, we had to content ourselves with looking at pictures of decorated trees in story books or imagining ourselves at the foot of those gift laden trees as in the few movies we saw. But we always could look to enjoy the beautifully decorated trees each Christmas season in our church.

The trees in church were very simply, yet beautifully, decorated with blue lights to resemble the stars over the manger scene.. We would get close to them, close enough to smell their heavy pine fragrance and picture the great snowy mountain top from where they might have come. When we sat up in the front pews, we would count the small cones among the thick branches and look to see where a bird's nest might have been before the tree was cut down.

For that matter, not only did we not have a Christmas tree but we did not have Christmas cards, gifts, lights, ornaments, mangers, Santas or the other figures that were displayed during this season. This is somewhat surprising, since our store always sold Christmas trees.

Our parents considered Christmas to be a holy time to be celebrated with Old Country traditions. Somber Advent led up to Christmas Day, when the holiday celebration commenced and culminated with the Feast of the Three Kings, Epiphany. Highlights of the celebrations with family and friends were the preparing of and later enjoyment of the many special foods made for these occasions.

Christmas trees in those years were not set up until the very night of Christmas Eve. During the Christmas season the outside of the store was banked with about a dozen wonderful smelling evergreen trees. Some sold for as little as 50 cents, but even that was a lot of money for many families trying to survive the depression era. Most families could only spend money for food and the barest of necessities.

The trees were brought each year on the big delivery trucks of John Graff's Wholesale Fruit and Produce, a local company. Father would sell them, but we never had a tree for our own celebration. Most of the time the trees were all sold, and if they were not, my parents most likely were too tired to think of one more thing to do, late on Christmas Eve. There was no time or energy other than for the preparation and enjoyment of our traditional Christmas Eve supper.

We always remembered to have some food ready to share with a poor hungry stranger who might be passing by, or for the Child Jesus who it is said roamed the world that special holy night, and who just might stop at our home some Christmas Eve. In contrast, today it is traditional to leave cookies and milk for Santa.

However, we did hear of Befana, the just witch, who gave disobedient children stones instead of gifts for Christmas. We also shared stories, especially on Epiphany, or Russian Christmas that some of our neighborhood friends celebrated on January 6, the day before my birthday! So it was, that whenever we had a Christmas tree, I tried to keep it at least until my birthday, and many times we did just that.

The December preceding my sixth birthday, my older sister and two older brothers kept asking Father about putting up a tree of our own at home. They heard of a few families that could afford to decorate a tree every year They remembered scenes from movies of gaily decorated trees, pictures in story books and wished to have one, too.

Finally, after much pleading, they were given permission to take one of the trees that had not sold yet to use for our very first Christmas tree. There were only two trees left. After a short and excited conference, my older sister and brothers decided on the taller of the two.

That tree was about 7' tall, still fresh but quite pathetic in appearance with very irregular and sparse branches. The trunk was as crooked as it could be yet still be called a tree.   Perhaps it should have been ground up for mulch.   But, we were as excited as could be. Finally, we were going to have a Christmas tree of our very own.   That fact alone made us feel this was a very nice tree.

Two pieces of wood were found and nailed cross fashion to the bottom of the tree to make it stand.   Since it was such a lop-sided tree, it took much time for Father and my older brothers to get it to stand as it should.   Several extra branches gathered from the yard were put here and there on the tree to help fill in the bare spots.   A white sheet was put about its base.   Lux soap flakes were scattered over that to simulate sparkling snow flakes.

Somebody was able to talk my Father into giving them some change and they quickly ran to the 5 and 10 cent store to buy a roll of red crepe paper and a packet of silver icicles. The crepe paper was draped as far as it would go across the front portion of the tree that was most visible as one walked into the room and the icicles were placed carefully about the tree. I even got to put a few icicles on; only a very few, near the bottom, because my older sister and brothers took first dibs on this happy job. All the paper decorations that were made at school were put here and there on the tree.

My older sister fashioned a paper star and stretched out some cotton to resemble snow for the top of the tree. We laughed with excitement, and I clapped for joy, as we watched our oldest brother climb the ladder to place that star at the very top of this now beautiful, we imagined, beautiful tree. Dancing around it and singing carols every other minute, we thought near the tree was the place to be.

Even though it was not our parent's custom to give gifts, one year my sister and brothers changed that too. They pleaded with Father for some money for gifts. He finally settled on five dollars. With that, my sister bought something for everyone from the 5 and 10 cents store For me there was a small 8" doll dressed in a blue knit outfit.

Some time around New Year's Day, Mother noticed the rapidly dropping needles and several times suggested that the tree had served its time and should be put out in the back yard for the birds to enjoy. We pleaded to keep it up a bit longer, then longer. It was up many days after most of the needles had dropped from its branches. The children of our family, not daring to dream there would ever be another one, hated to give up this much loved tree.

Sometimes, it seems like it all happened only yesterday, though it was so long ago. Despite greatly improved living conditions, the latest modern technology, the chemicals that have been added to our trees so that they stay up for days and days, memories of my own growing family and the homes we have lived in about the country; there's still a special spot in my heart for that first, most beautiful, lop-sided Christmas tree.

Chapter XIV

Closure

Destruction of our childhood neighborhood was completed years later, after my parents were both dead.   The community became involved in more property grabbing through the government's claim of eminent domain under the guise of an Urban Renewal Program.   Evidently the local "powers that be" decided to steam-roll any opposition to their actions, to stifle any objection.   Legal road blocks were everywhere.

Local officials had already made an agreement to sell all the properties in our part of town, including my father's store, to a local business man for a predetermined sum.   Our store property was within eyesight of the Interstate and only a short distance from the interchange.   It was some of the best real estate in the county.   Since the death of my father ten years earlier (Mother proceeding him), the property had been locked in probate court due to the indifference of family members still in the area.

I was married, living many miles away in another state and unaware of the situation until it was too late. The government found it to their benefit not to meet with owners in a timely fashion nor discuss or suggest alternatives. For us it was not Renewal but rather another funeral. I traveled back and forth many times for many months trying to right this wrong. But there were too many others skilled in this land grabbing game, having done it before, over and over.

It seemed foolish to take a stand against such an agency so experienced in robbing the public. I did try everything I could think of, even asking to let me buy back, what we already owned—our own property—for more than the government would be selling it for, or for what we were to receive from its sale. I found they had promised our property to someone else and we were told we now had no rights nor anything else to say about it. Was this the United States of America?

I convinced my surviving siblings to stand up to the government agency. However, many of the local attorneys claimed to be involved with work for the government's program and would not take our opposing suit because of "conflict of interest" rules. It was difficult to find a trustworthy attorney in the area. The first attorney we hired had a partner working for the agency. The next attorney we hired seemed to want to work for the agency.

While my parents lived, the tax assessor had rated the property at a rather large value with the consequentially large tax burden. But when the assessor for the agency sought to confiscate the land, his estimate of the property's value was but a small fraction of the amount my father had been taxed for in the days of the Depression. And now, it should have been even higher of course.

To the relief of the government agency, our final attorney (from another county) never called on me to testify in court. Somehow or other, I would have surely said what they would not have wanted anyone to hear. For one thing, we were told that if the tax comparison was made, a mistrial would have been declared. We were told, later, one young juror did understand that we were being robbed and fought long for us. But he was over ruled by the rest of the jury and so we were awarded an insulting pittance, slightly more than the offer made by the agency.

After the government took our property as well as all the other properties, the entire block was leveled and cleared. New sidewalks and public utilities were installed at taxpayer expense. All this was then given to a local businessman for less per square yard than you would pay for the cheapest carpeting. This "good" citizen now flies the US flag on the property all the time. Local officials had favored this same man a few years earlier with a similar deal, right in the center of town. They used our legal system to steal from their neighbors - unbelievable but true.

We had gone to court but lost a lopsided fight. Of course the money received as a result of the condemnation process paid our attorney's fee and court costs, leaving but a pittance to the family estate. Of the portion coming to me I gave part to my ailing Godmother, long since widowed, and the rest to a nephew. Not one cent of that corrupt money could I keep for myself.

Godmother had sacrificed quite an amount when she sold her income property to help my Father save our store from the Sheriff's sale. I still shudder to think where we would have ended up if she had not helped. The little I gave my Godmother could not make up for the difference she had lost, by any means; but I wanted to do this bit at least.

To this day, it is upsetting to think of anything that has to do with this town, county and government that allowed these terrible injustices to happen. It is even more difficult to reflect on the people who stirred up the mess and who continue to stir. I feel there is no reason for me to return to that area except to visit the graves of my parents and family.

Chapter XV

Epilogue

Sometimes I think of what else might have been done by our family during the Depression era. This must have been a traumatic time for our proud parents. Their great expectations were crushed by adversity and often they faced the future despairingly. We all suffered with them; but willingly took personal responsibility for doing all we could to assure our survival as a family. Without our parents having to say so, we knew there was never money for more than the barest necessities. We knew that many nights they were totally exhausted and had little time to help us. Even if they didn't verbalize their love for us, we knew they surely did love us, because of all they did for us even with their tremendous burdens and struggles.

Today's parents are advised that they must tell their children, in almost every other sentence, that they love them. Certainly that is fine, but for some reason, many children are given too many luxuries - more than the kings of old who possessed many worldly luxuries could even imagine. Why then is the world seeing far greater problems with unruly and violent children, who seem not to care for even the simplest of responsibilities? What devious devil has their hearts and souls?

Many modern children feel they never have or get enough; taking what they want and giving almost nothing in return. Honor and respect is something they do not give, yet they expect people to grovel before them. A good dose of humility and understanding, accompanied by the words: "Thank You" for whatever they receive would be more beneficial to all concerned. Rather, they give a display of anger for what they feel they should have gotten, yet, for whatever reason, didn't receive. Feeling surely deserving in all respects, they show hostility and contempt for parents who couldn't or wouldn't satisfy their desires.

We did what we could at home and also did well in school as evidenced by the number of times we were on the Honor Rolls. This we did without any help from our parents with our assignments. I didn't know that parents ever helped with homework. None of the children in our family felt any bitterness or placed blame on our parents at anytime for what we did not have nor get, emotionally or otherwise.

We have today more of the "good things" and a much easier life than our parents; a life they deserved more than we. It is sad to see so many people who think they are deprived, in today's world with its many excesses. They think they are having a tough time, become bitter, and point blame at others, or society, rather than accept their own personal responsibility.

At times I would like to have my parents back to enjoy the life of today with us. Undoubtedly, they would be amazed at all the wonderful things we have; but I am certain they would quickly be saddened and dismayed by the strange divergence from goodness in the world about us.

To all I wish much joy, peace and health;
The kindness of Family and Friends.
And may you always enjoy
Some kind of a lovely tree
With your loved ones,
At the Christmas times of your lives.

And now, there follow two stories that I would
like to share - one as a mother -
the other as a grandmother.

Chapter XVI

Warm Fluffy Christmas Sleepers

Many Christmas Eves ago, a family with three little children waited for their happy Christmas Day. They had moved to the town of South Bend, Indiana just three months before. Now at this holiday season the children, who missed their friends from their last home in Ithaca, New York, missed them even more. It was the Fall of 1955 when Father came to teach at the University of Notre Dame in this northern mid-western town, but the cost of the move had used up most of the money which Mother and he had saved over the years.

A very small, inexpensive house was found to rent, until they were able to afford something larger. Their parents spent many long days and nights scrubbing, painting and fixing the little cottage. It soon was so clean and pretty that everyone who saw it loved it.

In preparation for Christmas, the children helped Mother gather pine cones and fresh evergreen branches from their yard to decorate the front door and the living room. Handmade paper decorations and the collections from holidays past were carefully added. All this was done to prepare for the day they would soon celebrate: Christmas, the birth of the baby Jesus.

Mother and Father were happy to see that their children loved everything about Christmas as much as they did. Older Sister and Brother constantly sang and talked about the wonders of the season. As they skipped about the little cottage, Baby Sister crawled happily behind them. She felt the excitement, too. It was so hard to wait for Christmas.

The radio and record player sang out the beautiful carols about the birth of Christ as well as songs and stories of the season. Many were about Santa, of course. Santa had already come to visit them at a Christmas party at their church. Out of his great big bag, he had given each child an orange, a candy cane and a small box of candy. The box of candy had pictures of snow scenes and of Santa, himself. A white shoestring handle was used to carry the box. Inside there were hard candies and a chocolate covered cream drop. Um-mm, so good. Then, Santa listened carefully to what each child wanted for Christmas.

The children's mother knew there was very little money to spend for extra wishes this Christmas so she cautioned the children that it was best to "just expect a few surprises." Since most of the family's money had been used to pay for the move to Indiana and for paint, plaster and putty to make the run-down rental suitable for their young family, more money would still be needed for the extra coal to keep them warm this very long, cold winter.

Mother knew how cold the children would be as winter deepened. Most of all, she longed to see them able to go to sleep on Christmas Eve in new, warm, footed sleepers. The only pairs of pajamas the children now owned were not only too small, but also too thin, faded and worn out at the knees. But, if she bought them new ones before Christmas, there would be almost no money for anything else. She thought of how nice it would be if only Santa could bring sleepers to them before bedtime on Christmas Eve instead of on Christmas morning. But how? Everyone knows Santa only comes after everyone is snug in their beds, soundly asleep. Still, Mother thought and hoped and prayed.

Thankfully, a very much appreciated surprise of some money came as a gift to help University families have a better Christmas. This gift was from the University at the request of their new, young President, Father "Ted" Hesburgh. How grateful Mother was for such help. Now, with this gift, Mother knew she could buy some of the traditional holiday foods they would all share and still something extra for the three children. Otherwise, it would not have been possible to have enough money left to buy the extra things little boys and girls dream about and hope to see under their tree on Christmas morning.

All that Christmas Eve afternoon, radio programs were being interrupted with progress reports of Santa's trip. First, Santa and his reindeer were spotted on Air Force radar leaving the North Pole. Later he was seen over Alaska, then Northern Canada, and next it was Mid-Canada. On and on they flew on their merry rounds. They were getting closer and closer to Indiana and the little house. The children grew more excited as they listened to these reports. But at supper time, to some protest from Santa's little followers, Father turned the radio off so as to have a peaceful supper on this special night.

The family enjoyed a traditional candlelight Christmas Eve supper of hot borscht (a red beet soup - topped with a dollop of white sour cream). Borscht, as well as herring, was one of their Father's family traditions for Christmas Eve supper. It was followed by some of Mother's traditions.

Two small bowls were filled with angel hair pasta. One bowl was buttered for the children to share. The other bowl of pasta had a sauce of minced garlic lightly cooked in hot olive oil, mixed with some mashed anchovies and a little water. This was topped with several whole anchovies and grated cheese for the grownups. There was also a salad, and on a white platter, a wreath of steamed broccoli decorated with red pimento.

Then . . . just before dessert, there was a *LOUD POUNDING* on the front door; so loud and hard that it shook their dear little home. Brother and Sister ran to the door, flung it open but saw . . no one there. Pretty white snow was falling quietly all around. They knew they'd heard the sound of something. Was it the wind whirling above the rooftop or was it the sound of something else?

Oh! Oh! What was that beside the door?

They became very excited when they saw A BIG WHITE BOX tied with fat, red yarn. Their eyes widened and danced with joy as, together, they carried the BIG BOX to the kitchen. Baby Sister, sitting in her high chair, clapped her hands with glee. There was a note on top of the box - and - it was from Santa!

The children became more excited as Mother read the note! Santa's note said he would be back later to fill the children's stockings. Like Mother, Santa wanted the children to be sleeping in nice, new, warm, fluffy sleepers on Christmas Eve. So, he had decided to make this special trip to their little house with the new sleepers and promised to make his regular stop after everyone was sound asleep, snug in their beds. Oh, how nice and wonderful! Mother's dream had come true!

The children had early baths, put on their new, warm, fluffy sleepers, and then said special prayers of thanks. Father and Mother hugged and kissed them goodnight and tucked them into their beds. Even as excited as they were, the children soon fell happily asleep in cuddly pink, blue and yellow sleepers. They dreamed sweet dreams until early Christmas morn.

When they awoke, they could smell the delicious aroma of the pancakes Mother was cooking in the kitchen. In the living room, Father had a cheerful, warm fire crackling in the fireplace where they quickly gathered. to start this day of wonders. Sure enough, Santa had come again as he promised. He had put fruit, nuts, sweets and a few coins in their stockings. Under their little evergreen tree were two small dolls, one for each of the girls, and a little toy car for their brother. They each got a picture book from Santa, too. Truly, this would be a happy, memorable Christmas after all, smiled Mother.

As the years went by, two more boys were born to this family. For these five children, Santa has repeated the sleeper trip many, many, many Christmas Eves, even after the children were grown and married. Although they moved about the country, Santa always found them wherever they were - from New Jersey to California and from Michigan to Florida. The littlest children wondered how he knew where to find them when they moved to new homes. On one of Santa's visits to the shopping center, the youngest child asked him how he could do this. She was worried, for the family had just moved and he probably didn't have their new address.

Santa told the children that he has teams of special elves with one of the most important jobs at the North Pole. All day long, these elves do nothing else but walk up and down giant address books as big as the floor to change or add new addresses. That is how Santa always knew when and to where the children moved, even after they were grown. He knew all the right sizes and just how many sleepers to bring for the little ones in each family every Christmas Eve.

And Mother is so very happy about all this, for her five children married and now had children of their own. Today, as a Grandmother, she shares these warm, lovely Christmas Eve dreams with ten good grandchildren!

For my 10 good grandchildren: Andrew, Adam, Charles, Alexander, Erica, Anastasia, Nicholas, Christopher, Jessica, and Karen; and their parents who first lived this story

A MERRY GOOD CHRISTMAS
TO ALL!

Chapter XVII

A Fond Farewell or A Cousins' Party

Grandparents Stan and Rose planned a Cousins' Farewell party for Cousins Adam and Erica who, together with their parents, were moving from Florham Park, New Jersey to Naperville, Illinois so that their Father could start his new job in Chicago.

Spring was now here, the first weekend of April, 1991 in New Providence, NJ. It was nothing less than glorious, the flowers and trees were blooming, and the weather couldn't have been more perfect. The day would have been simply flawless if only cousin Nicholas from Indiana had been with them in person. He was missed by all but remained in everyone's thoughts. We also missed his Mom and Dad who were at their home back in Indiana.

It all started on Friday afternoon when Aunt Rosemary from Cincinnati, Ohio drove up in her van carrying her sons, Cousins Andy and Charlie; with their Aunt Marianne and her children, Cousins Alex and Ana; all together. Uncle David (Andy and Charlie's Dad) stayed in Ohio, Uncle Phil (Alex and Ana's Dad) in Pennsylvania and Adam and Erica's Dad, Tom, was in Illinois doing grownup things.

Friday night, Aunt Marianne used Grandma Rose's toppings - meatballs, black olives, pepperoni and mozzarella cheese - to make the best Cousins' pizzas.

While the Cousins waited for the pizzas to be baked, they sat at the dining room table covered with very long rolls of plain white shelf paper as their placemats. They all had many crayons. Each Cousin colorfully decorated the rolled out paper where they were sitting, while chatting about things young cousins do. They drank from personalized glass mugs that their Granddad Stan had painted for them, using these for each meal throughout this special Cousins' weekend.

Nibbles were carrots, celery slivers and whole olives, the black ones and the stuffed ones. No one, however, asked for broccoli, mushrooms or spinach. Appetites were finally quenched by ice cream with any possible topping one could think of. There were chocolate and butterscotch syrups; berries, cherries, colored sugars, chocolate sprinkles, butterscotch or chocolate chips, bananas and of course, whipped cream to put on top of the syrup. There was even a nice plate of Aunt Marianne's super chocolate chip cookies to make everyone so much happier.

The boys then retreated into the garage to play with toy cars and card games while telling all about their many adventures. Erica and Ana went through the closets upstairs in the bedrooms to find just the right clothes to use for play dress-up. They giggled and whispered and twirled and danced about the rooms. They put on a great fashion and style show for the grownups. It was such fun.

Anastasia   Erica

All were enjoying themselves but bedtime, 10:30 pm, for this party came incredibly fast. Soon though, under Grandmother Rose's care, all six happy Cousins were in the third floor bedrooms

(Peanut Heaven). They said their prayers and soon were sound asleep, dreaming their own private dreams.

Morning found them up early, all bright eyed and bushy tailed, anxious to enjoy many more things together. They could smell the wonderful pancakes that Granddad was cooking for them. While they waited for their stack of cakes, they again continued the coloring of the long placemats and chatted about the plans for the day. Before long, they had been fed totally and fully with orange and apple juices, pancakes, sausages and Aunt Rosemary's apple sauce.

Granddad Stan piled them all into his van and sped the six little Cousins to the nearby Watchung Reservation. There they looked for deer, swung on swings, ran through the woods, skipped stones on the lake, climbed trees and other things. Then someone spotted this strange tree and climbing up one by one they all found their favorite location. Granddad thought it looked great and took their picture.

Since the three youngest were tired and now ready to go back to their Grandfather's house, he called Aunt Marianne from a phone at the shelter house asking her to drive up and take them back. Granddad then took Andy, Adam and Alex for a long hike to the Dam at the end of Surprise Lake.

It was a really long, long hike. They saw many fallen trees, people on horse back, groups of joggers, the animals of the forest, and a man driving a sulky cart with a fringe on top.

They rested and skipped stones across Surprise
Lake before starting back to rejoin their families.

Meanwhile, back at the house, everyone was busy getting the front and back patios set up for the next Cousins' event. Later that afternoon, Cousins Christopher and Jessica came with their parents and brought large packages of Popsicles in all the flavors anyone could think of. Even though all the Cousins had one of each flavor, there were still a few left.

Granddad then started a fire in the outdoor brick fireplace where the children toasted hotdogs and marshmallows. Granddad cooked hamburgers and corn on the cob in the big fireplace. Grandmother Rose had Polish sausage and sauerkraut, potato salad, Aunt Rosemary's pickles, tomato preserves, pickled beets and varied fruits for all to enjoy. There still was no demand for broccoli, mushrooms or spinach.

Lots of videos were taken of the hubbub and of the musical treasure hunt made up by Aunt Rosemary. Baby Jessica had lots of fun just watching everyone. The treasure hunt started up on the third floor (Peanut Heaven); the Cousins then came down through the house, stopping at this place and that, looking for and finding many clues.

Next they looked outdoors, to the front and to the back of the house, in and out of the Cousins' Clubhouse that had all their names painted above the door. They checked around trees and around the big, brick outdoor fireplace. Now, they went back into the house to the laundry room where Chris found the last clue.

Chris found the treasure in the dryer! It was a large bag filled with toys, coins and other goodies for each of the treasure hunters. Everyone liked the treasures that Grandmother Rose had packed for each Cousin.

When the treasure hunt was over, they looked at a video made from old time movies taken of their Moms and Dads when they were as young as the Cousins. It was hard to believe that their great big parents had been so small once.

Chris and Jessica went home with their parents as the rest of us went to the 5 PM Mass at Our Lady of Peace Church a few blocks from home. We sat in the front pews and Ana and Erica fell asleep during the sermon and kept on sleeping through out the rest of the Mass.

After church was over, we all drove to Adam and Erica's house in Florham Park where Aunt Lisa served her super chili, salad AND homemade rice crispy squares. It was the last of many wonderful visits to this house because Adam and Erica moved a few days later to Illinois where their Dad had started to work at his new job.

All the cousins played in the back yard while it grew darker and darker until a million stars shone extra brightly that night. Regretfully we knew it was time for us to leave Adam and Erica so that all the Cousins could get some much needed sleep. There were many hugs and kisses all around with sad good-byes. But, we knew there would be other wonderful get-togethers of these great girls and boys.

Sunday morning soon came and it was more of a grown up kind of day. Uncle Phil arrived from Pennsylvania early in the morning and was able to have breakfast with us. He stayed until after Sunday dinner and then drove Cousins Alex, Ana and their Mother (Aunt Marianne) back to their home in Lewisburg. It took them about three hours to get back to their home, tired but happy to be sure.

Cousins Andy, Charlie and their Mother stayed with their Grandparents Stan and Rose until Tuesday when their Mom sadly said they had to leave for their home in Cincinnati, Ohio.

Grandmother Rose especially liked this gathering. She remembers all her happy grandchildren, their parents, the delicious food, the games, the fun of playing cards, every day with all the Cousins on the front patio under the big table umbrella. There were games like Fish, War, Hearts, Kings in the Corner, and others. She enjoyed them all even though she hardly ever won. All the Cousins are pretty good at card games it seems. How colorful and busy the back yard and back patio were with all the games, talking and eating of special foods.

Now, it is all a memory, this wonderful weekend, and we hope it was a very good one for all the Cousins and their parents. Grandmother dreams of more times like these whenever these Cousins and their parents get together, to enjoy each other's company, with good food and good times.

This is cousin Karen who was not yet born at the time of the party

Cousins Chris and Jessica came too late
to climb trees

This is cousin Nicholas who lived too far away to
come to the party.

* * * *

Grandmother Rose sends love and good wishes to her dear, treasured grandchildren; these Cousins and to all Cousins everywhere .